EINSTEIN
PUZZLES

EINSTEIN
PUZZLES

BRAIN STRETCHING CHALLENGES
INSPIRED BY THE SCIENTIFIC GENIUS

DR. GARETH MOORE

All events, scenarios, and descriptions
contained herein are fictional and are in no way
intended to be taken as fact in relation to the
life and work of Albert Einstein.

This edition published in 2023 by Arcturus Publishing Limited
26/27 Bickels Yard, 151–153 Bermondsey Street,
London SE1 3HA

AD008187NT

Printed in the UK

CONTENTS

Introduction 7

Puzzles 9

Solutions 202

INTRODUCTION

There is a reason that "Einstein" is synonymous with "genius". His theories revolutionized the way we look at not just the world but the entire universe around us. In particular he developed the theory of special relativity, which predicted correctly how measurements of space, time, and mass change when moving at different speeds—an idea that is encapsulated by the famous equation, $E=mc2$. He also developed the theory of general relativity, explaining how gravity relates to other forces of nature. These two theories together form an overarching "theory of relativity", making Albert Einstein—despite his death many decades ago in 1955—the world's best-known physicist right up to the current day.

Although influenced by the work and life of Einstein, the situations described in this book are entirely fictional. Many of the questions are set in laboratories and research facilities, but you won't need any kind of scientific equipment to solve the puzzles in this book—just a sharp pencil, and an equally sharp mind. The puzzles are designed to be solved by a logical process of deduction combined with common sense, and there is a single, unique solution for each conundrum. The solution can always be deduced entirely from the information you have been given on the page, so as Einstein himself said, "The important thing is not to stop questioning".

From page 177 onwards, however, with the exceptions of pages 184-185, 190-193 and 200-201, the puzzles refer to actual, real-life scientific phenomena. For these questions you may prefer to approach them by making a reasoned, intelligent guess, based on what you already know about the natural world. No advanced scientific knowledge is required, since as Einstein himself once said, "The true sign of intelligence is not knowledge but imagination".

A full set of solutions can be found at the back of the book for you to check your answers, which also generally include an explanation as to how you could arrive at the given answer. If you have a friend nearby, you could even ask them to check the solution to a puzzle and give you a hint, if stuck, to help you get going—or of course you could try and crack the conundrum as a team. As Einstein put it, "Once we accept our limits, we go beyond them".

So put on your (hypothetical) goggles and lab coat, sharpen your pencil, and prepare to dive into Einstein's world of time and space—and puzzles.

PLAYING BALL

Two physicists at Einstein's research facility decided to play a game of tennis during their lunch break. When they reached the bottom floor of their office building, however, they realized they had left their tennis ball in their lab on the top floor.

Shouting up to their associate in the lab, the physicists asked if their friend could drop a tennis ball down to them, while avoiding the small stream that flowed directly beside the building. Unfortunately, however, the windows did not open and there was only a small opening to the outside, through a fume cupboard vent. This meant that the associate could only drop the ball vertically and not throw it outward.

How could the friend drop the ball in such a way that it would hopefully avoid falling directly downward into the stream?

HOT AND COLD

During a fluid dynamics experiment, a researcher needed to freeze a certain volume of water within a set time.

 The researcher poured water into a container, and weighed both the water and container together. The researcher ensured that there was sufficient space in the container for the water to expand by approximately 10% of its volume once frozen.

Given that the water and container weighed 650g before being frozen, what would be the resulting weight of the ice and container once it had completely frozen?

COMPARE AND CONTRAST

In a lab, an apprentice and a researcher were comparing two gold ingots.
The apprentice mismeasured both ingots, obtaining the following readings:

- Ingot A weighs 350g

- Ingot B weights 420g

The researcher checked the measurements, and observed that:

- Ingot A needs two-sevenths of its actual weight added to the previous reading

- Ingot B needs an an eighth of its actual weight added to the previous reading

Which ingot was heavier?

BOOKMARKED
FOR LATER

Einstein sat in a chair at the university library, watching two students of aerodynamics having a discussion about air resistance. Each student was reading a book, and both had bookmarks made of card to keep their places. One of the students nudged her bookmark off the table, and it fell downward and landed flat on the floor.

The second student placed a bet, as follows. If he could drop his own bookmark from the same height and make it land not flat on the floor but instead on its paper-thin edge, the first student would agree to proofread the second's thesis when it was complete—or vice versa, if he failed in this task. The first student readily accepted this seemingly unlikely bet.

What could the second student do to his bookmark to significantly increase the chance of it landing on one of its thin edges?

THE RESEARCH FACILITY

Four researchers had been resident in a remote research facility for six months. When viewed from above the building was a perfect square, with one large window in each wall, beneath which each scientist sat at a desk.

On first moving in, the scientists each installed a blind at their window to keep out the sun, even though all of the windows faced north. Six months later, however, they found that they did not need their blinds at all—not even at noon, when there were cloudless skies.

Where was the research facility?

HIDDEN SYMBOLS

As a scientist was handing over from her shift to her research partner, she mentioned that she had left a coded message on a desk in the lab they were both using.

Intrigued, the research partner found on his desk a scrap of paper on which the following had been written:

Carbon, Gold, Titanium,
Oxygen, Nitrogen

Can you decode the scrap of paper to reveal a one-word message?

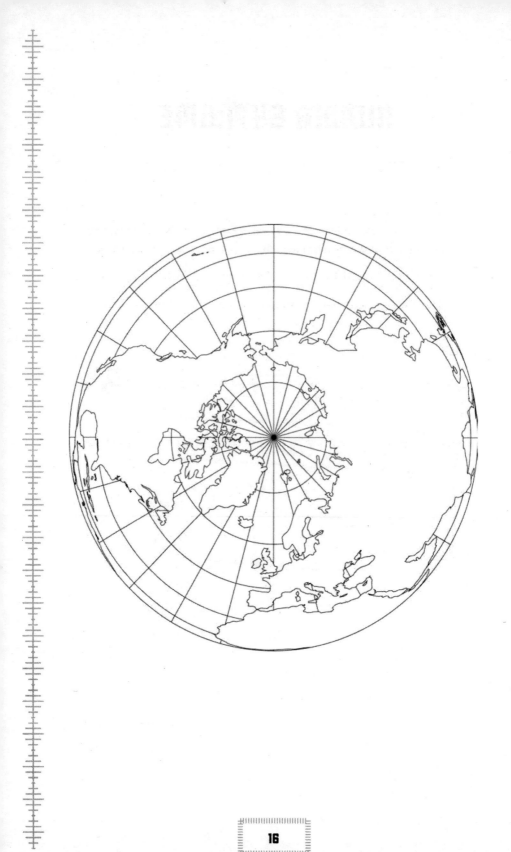

NOT AS EXTREME

A meteorologist was studying wind speeds around the North Pole, and took part in a circumpolar flight in order to progress some fieldwork.

- The plane took off and flew North for exactly 50 miles.

- The plane then turned eastward, and flew for 314 miles along an equal line of latitude.

- Next, the plane flew south for 50 miles.

- The plane landed, at the same airfield it originally took off from, which was not at the North Pole.

At what distance from the North Pole was the airfield, to the nearest mile?

TIME TRAVELS

A young astrophysicist with an interest in time travel had, at Einstein's recommendation, borrowed several library books, hoping to read more about the history of astronomy. With a solid grounding in the scientific thinking of the past, she felt that she would be more likely to be able to build toward greater breakthroughs in the future.

In one of the volumes, she read about the observations of an astronomer who had created several surprisingly accurate night-sky charts in 1442. In a different book, however, it was claimed that the same astronomer had created their first, less accurate, charts in 1478—a difference of 36 years.

The student was satisfied that both books were accurate, despite the earlier charts having been made in a seemingly later year, and that the astronomer involved had not used time travel to achieve the feat.

Why?

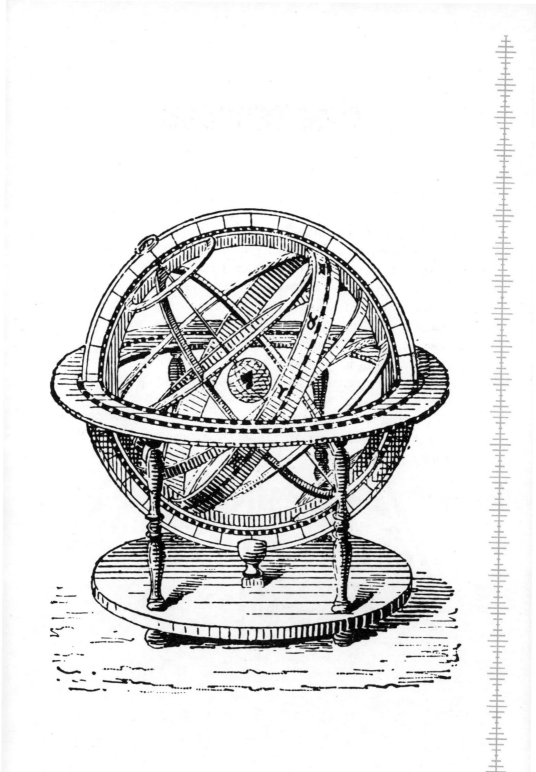

DISPERSION
DIVERSION

A student of fluid dynamics was performing an experiment that involved observing the dispersion of a pink liquid when poured into a clear liquid.

The student had two flasks: one filled with pink liquid, and the other filled with clear liquid. They poured a certain quantity of the pink liquid into the clear liquid, mixed it a little by giving it a gentle swirl, and then poured the same quantity of the resulting mixed liquid back into the original pink flask. This meant that both flasks now contained the same quantity of liquid as each had had at the start.

A second student, watching this experiment, observed that there must now be the same quantity of pink liquid in the clear flask as there would be clear liquid in the pink flask. But the first student argued that it was impossible to know that this was true, especially given how crudely the two had been mixed together.

Which student was correct?

THE GUEST LIST 1

At a scientific conference that Einstein was attending, a list of speakers had been printed for attendees to review.

To his great amusement, he noticed that, on a particular panel, all of the speakers' initials happened to form chemical symbols—all except for one, that is:

Kaitlyn Ross   Olivia Green

Ben Hall   Phoebe Ingles

Pete Benitez   Zara Reynolds

Selena Evans   Xanthe Estefan

Which speaker is the odd one out?

TEST CUBES

A structural engineer was comparing two perfect cubes, each made of a different metal. For the sake of clarity, he identified one as cube A and the other as cube B.

- Cube A was made of a metal that was known to have a density four times the density of the metal used to make cube B, meaning it weighed four times as much for a piece of the same volume.

- Cube B was twice the size of Cube A, in every dimension—width, height, and depth.

Which cube was heavier, and by how much?

THE DARK SIDE

A young niece of Einstein's had set up her telescope so that she could study the moon. She planned to take photographs of the moon's surface every day for a year, in order to create a complete survey of its topography.

   When she next met up with her uncle, however, he told her that no matter how many photographs she took from her position, she would only ever be able to photograph half of the moon's surface.

Why would this be?

THE OBSERVERS OBSERVE

Around thirty students of logic were gathered together in a library. Several of them were asleep.

The group regularly studied together, and naps were a common occurrence. One of the awake students said to another:

"There's always one person in this group for whom it's true that if they are napping, everybody is napping."

Could the logistician always be correct?

STUDENT AND SUPERVISOR

A supervisor and her student are clearing up after their latest experiment. They are each washing beakers at a constant rate per beaker, although the student is more careful and it takes him more time to wash beakers.

Together, it takes them 21 minutes to wash all of the beakers from their experiment.

If the supervisor had acted alone, however, it would have taken her 28 minutes to wash all of the beakers.

How long would it have taken the student to wash all of the beakers, at his own constant rate?

TWO ROVERS

Two rovers are exploring an outer planet of the solar system, and come across a circular liquid lake. To investigate further, one of the rovers sends a floating probe into the lake to retrieve a sample to analyze its contents, but it floats away from the rover and—maybe due to the currents in the lake—stops moving once it reaches the middle of the lake. The rovers can clearly see its transmission mast standing tall in the middle.

The two rovers are not equipped to enter the liquid to retrieve the probe. The two rovers, however, can be tethered together with a cord of a length that happens to be just over twice the distance from the edge of the lake to the lost probe.

How could the two rovers retrieve the probe, without entering the liquid?

THE DRAG RACE

Two of Einstein's colleagues had created a driverless solar-powered car, which they wanted to test out. They set up a straight course, which was exactly two miles in length.

They ensured that the vehicle was sufficiently charged, and set it on a straight course. They had observed that the car covered the first mile in one minute, but with each subsequent minute it covered only half of the distance it had completed in the previous minute.

Assuming the car moved in a straight line toward the finish, at the rate described, how long would it take for the car to complete the 2-mile test course?

FRENCH CORRECTION

Einstein once related with amusement the story of a renowned French astronomer who had set up a telescope at the top of the Eiffel Tower in December, after being given special dispensation to leave it there for a period of a full six months.

The astronomer returned each night to monitor the skies from the telescope, but he noticed that his readings were becoming less and less accurate over time, with considerable drift from his original sightings. In fact, after six months, the telescope seemed to have risen notably higher above sea level than its initial position, despite measurements showing that the ground level had not risen at all. This confused the astronomer, and he was unable to explain the discrepancies from an astronomical point of view.

Einstein himself then correctly predicted that, if left until December, the telescope would eventually return to its original position above sea level.

How can you explain the phenomenon?

SET THEORY 1

A chemist has sketched the following three groupings in his notebook:

Set A
Methane

Ammonia

Set B
Carbon dioxide

Quicklime

Set A + B
Water

Ethanol

Can you work out what classification rules he might have used for each of the sets, in order to sort the compounds in this way?

As a chemist, he was familiar with the chemical formula for each of the compounds.

MAJESTIC MECHANICS

To his great amusement, Einstein received through the mail some samples of a certain coin that featured his face on one side.

He placed two of these identical coins flat on a table, with one touching the top of the other as shown below. In particular he placed each coin with the head the right way up, as shown, and the face looking to the right.

Einstein then began to roll the top coin around the bottom one in a clockwise motion.

How far around the bottom coin would the top coin have rotated before the two faces were directly looking at one another?

FLUID DYNAMICS

Two students of fluid dynamics had each designed a clock that functioned like an hourglass as the liquid flowed through, but each had used a liquid of a different viscosity.

After testing, their fluid clocks were reported to behave as follows:

- For all of the liquid to pass through clock A took exactly 4 minutes

- For all of the liquid to pass through clock B took exactly 9 minutes

Without using any other equipment, and without guessing, how could they use their two fluid hourglasses to measure a time of exactly one minute?

DRIP FEEDING 1

A chemist set up a row of flasks so that she might examine the relative corrosiveness of an acid at different concentrations.

Each flask in the row had the same volume of acid poured into it, and then the chemist diluted the acids by adding different volumes of distilled water to each flask.

The first flask had one drop of water added, the second had two drops of water added, the third three, and so on.

She took exactly one second to administer each drop of water, and it took her a total of two minutes to fill all her flasks.

How many drops of water were in the most-diluted flask?

GROWING PAINS

An engineer at Einstein's research facility was testing out a lamp which they believed could improve the growing conditions of plants in otherwise minimal light conditions.

After monitoring the growth of a particular bamboo shoot, the engineer noticed that the rate of growth was increasing over time. In fact, the bamboo shoot was tripling in size every day.

Given that the bamboo shoot was 10cm tall when the experiment began, how many days (i.e. periods of 24 hours) would it take for the shoot to reach the ceiling of the test lab, which was 8m above the level of the soil in which the shoot had been planted?

SEEING CLEARLY

One of Einstein's assistants was stocking up on safety goggles for one of the laboratories that he frequented.

Unfortunately, the assistant accidentally ordered more pairs than were needed. When they arrived, he discovered that all but 16 of the new goggles could fit into their designated cabinet, which was previously empty.

The chemist then found an alternative empty cabinet to store the goggles in, which he noted could hold 40% more goggles than the previous cabinet. In fact, it could hold all of the new goggles, without any space left over.

How many goggles had the assistant ordered?

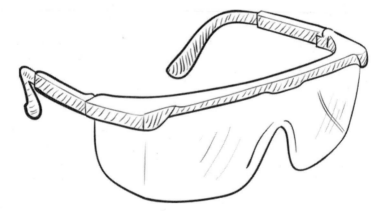

A SOLUTION

A lab technician was mixing ordinary table salt and water to create a solution which was 99% water and 1% salt, and which filled a 1l beaker.

The technician had made a mistake, however, and it turned out that he needed the solution to be 2% salt.

As they had at this point unfortunately run out of salt, the technician simply heated the beaker gently until enough of the solution had evaporated to satisfy him that it now consisted of 98% water and 2% salt.

By how much had the weight of the resulting solution decreased, relative to that of the full 1l beaker?

ARTIFICIAL INTELLIGENCE

A team of robotics engineers had, after several years of research, created a robot which they believed was capable of near-human intelligence. In case of malfunction, however, it was fastened to a tether which it was neither able to sever or unplug from itself.

The robot was placed on one side of a large lab, and the computer that oversaw its control was placed 10m away on the opposite side of the same lab.

One day, an engineer entered the room to discover that the robot had managed to cross over to the opposite side of the room, reach the control computer, and shut itself down.

Given that the tether cable was only 3m in length, how had the robot been able to cross the room, with the cord still attached to it?

NATURAL RESISTANCE

Einstein was reading through the latest scientific literature when he came across the following experiment, involving two flights that were aiming to test the theory of relativity by both taking off and landing at the same airport with no stops in between.

The first flight circumnavigated the globe in an easterly direction, while the second flight was almost identical to the first except that the plane flew in a westerly direction around the world while otherwise still using the same route as the first flight. The plane maintained a constant power for both flights.

There had, however, been a constant easterly wind throughout both flights, creating a headwind for the first flight and then a tailwind for the second flight. So, at a later date, the entire experiment—both flights—was repeated when there was no wind at all for the entirety of both flights.

Which pair of flights took longer overall? The first pair of flights with a headwind and then tailwind, or the second pair of flights without any headwind or tailwind? Or did they have identical durations?

None of this had anything to do with the theory of relativity, Einstein noted, but it was still an interesting question to consider.

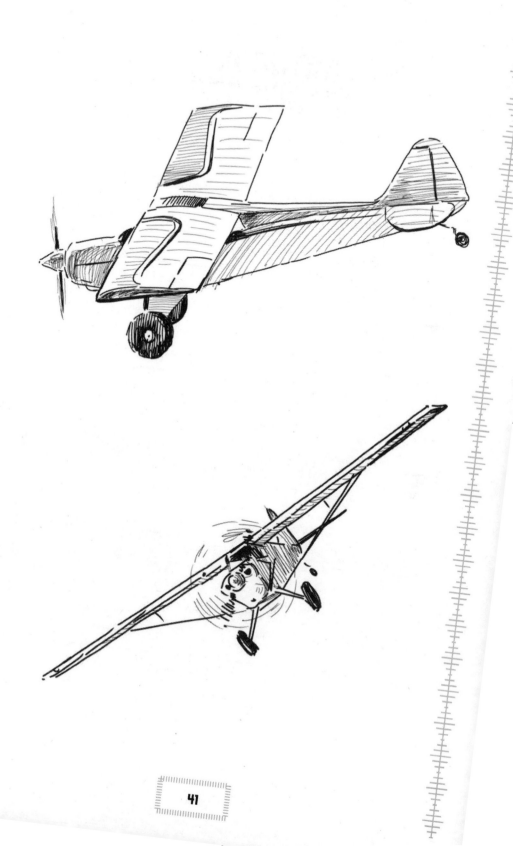

THE ATOMIC CLOCKS

The following report on an experiment involving atomic clocks was found lying around on a table at Einstein's research institute. Three of the key words had been left blank, however. Can you fill them in correctly?

Abstract

Three chemical elements were tested for use in atomic clocks. Each element had its accuracy as a timekeeping element assessed.

Method

A reference timer was started, using an existing atomic clock. One of the elements being tested was placed into the testing clock, and the reference time noted. After seven days, the testing clock time was compared against the current reference time and the difference noted. This was then repeat for the other two elements in turn.

In order to ensure the experiment was blind, each element was assigned a code name by a third party and then identified only by that name during the experiment.

Variables

Elements: caesium, mercury, rubidium
Code names: Mu, Tau, and Xi

Observations

- The caesium clock was the least precise

- The element code-named "Tau" was rubidium

- "Xi" gave the best precision

Results

1. The clock using _____ as an element, with code
    name _____, was the most precise.

2. The clock using caesium as an element, with code name
    _____, was the least precise.

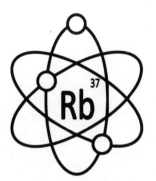

ATOMIC STRUCTURE

Suppose that a chemical element has a cubic crystalline structure, so that eight of its atoms would be arranged in the following way, where the small spheres represent individual atoms:

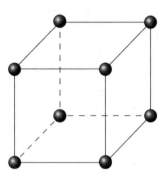

If this cubic arrangement is instead drawn as a solid block, for clarity, then the addition of four more atoms could result in the following picture that shows two cubes. This structure contains twelve atoms, of which ten are visible:

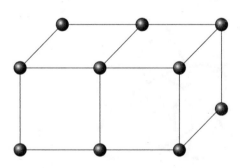

Assuming it has also been drawn in the same way, as if each cube were a solid block, then how many atoms are present in the following crystalline structure? Assume that the lowermost layer consists of a 3 × 3 arrangement of cubes with none extending further below.

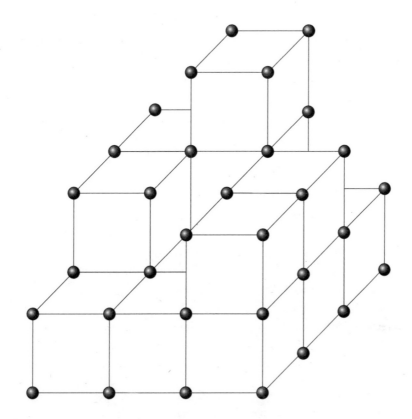

FAIR AND SQUARE

A mathematician had written out the following numerical sequence in a notebook:

7 2 14 11 5 4 12 13 3 6 10 15 1 8

He had deliberately written the numbers in a specific order, based on a certain piece of mathematical logic, although he could equally well have written the same list of numbers in reverse and exactly the same property would have applied.

As he reviewed the sequence, however, he realized that he had made an error when writing it down. He had intended to include all of the numbers from 1 to 15 in his list, but one was missing. Despite this, however, the intended logic still applied correctly throughout the entire list, and would do so when read in reverse too.

Where should the missing number be placed?

7 2 14 11
5 4 12 13
3 6 10 15
1 8

PRECISELY
THE POINT

A researcher working on Einstein's theory of special relativity was carrying out a survey of all of the doctoral candidates in her department.

First, she gathered as many of the doctoral candidates as she could and invited them into the cafeteria.

Second, once they were all there, she asked each of them in turn exactly the same scientific measurement question, requesting that they answer as accurately as they could using the available equipment within the room.

Each of the candidates answered correctly, even though each gave a different answer to the question.

What do you think the question was?

IN ALL PROBABILITY

Two researchers were examining the reactivity of metals, and had four small, sealed containers on a shelf. One contained sodium, another potassium, and the third and fourth containers contained lithium. All of the containers were identical in size.

One of the researchers selected two containers at random from the shelf, in order to test the contents. He noted that one of the containers held lithium.

What is the probability that he had picked two lithium containers from the shelf?

THE RUNNING TOTAL

A researcher is examining a collection of 100 incorrectly categorized fossils under a microscope, and attempting to correctly identify and re-label them all before an upcoming conference.

They work out that if they can manage to identify ten fossils a day—including on the first day of the conference—they will be able to complete the task in time.

After several days of hard work, however, they realize that they have only managed to identify the first fifty fossils they have examined, at a rate of five fossils per day—which is only half of the rate they required.

How many days do they have left to identify the remaining specimens?

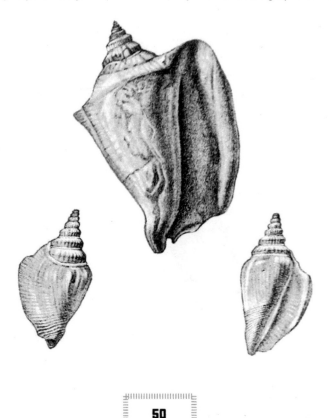

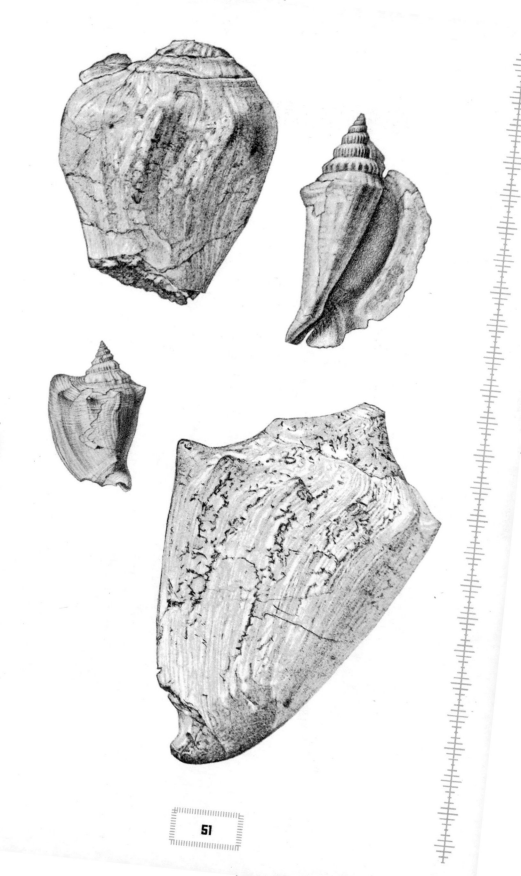

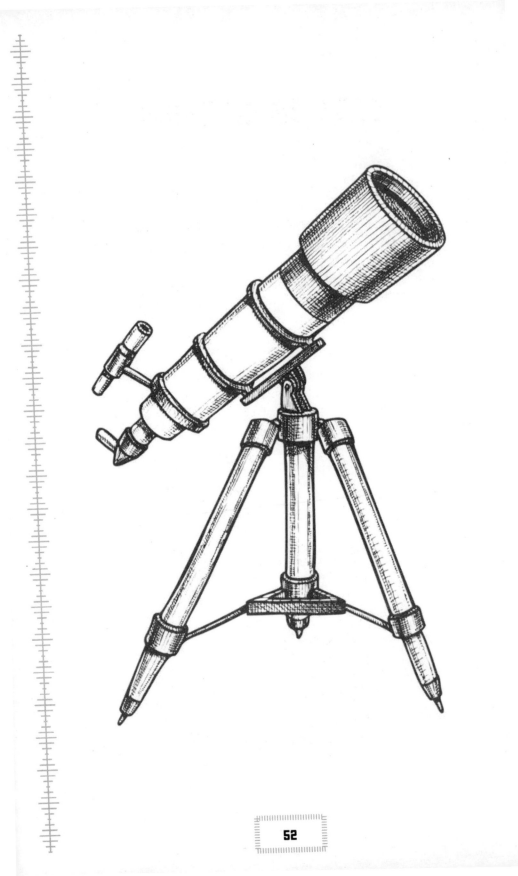

SETTING UP CAMP

A group of astronomers were helping to find evidence for Einstein's theory of relativity, so set up for a night's observation in an area with low light pollution.

Each of them had brought exactly one camping chair with them, and each chair had four legs. Each astronomer had also brought at least one telescope with them, and all telescopes were set on stands which had three legs.

While waiting for nightfall, a member of the group noted that the number of chairs plus the number of telescopes was equal to 16. They also noted that there 54 legs in total—excluding the legs of the astronomers themselves, so counting just the telescope stands and the camping chairs.

How many astronomers had set up camp, and how many telescopes were there?

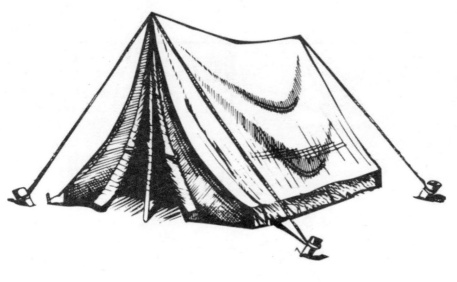

THE GUEST LIST 2

At a scientific conference where Einstein was the keynote speaker, workshop participants were invited to engage in an ice-breaker activity.

Guests were asked to pair up with another person in such a way that the first letters of the pair's given names could make up the symbol of a chemical element. George and Emma, for example, could pair up to create "Ge"—the symbol for Germanium.

Which two of these people would never be able to pair with anyone?

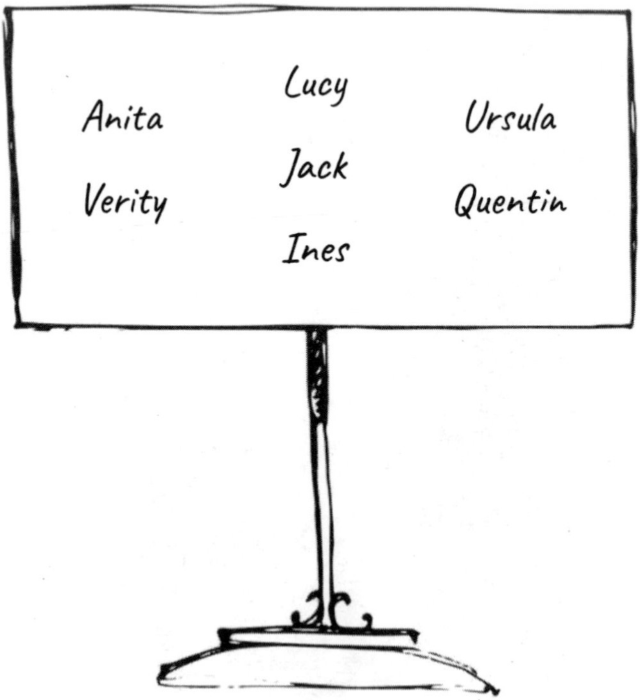

Anita

Lucy

Ursula

Verity

Jack

Quentin

Ines

THE LOWEST
OF THE LOW

A meteorologist was searching for a particularly robust thermometer to take with them on an Arctic expedition, where temperatures were expected to regularly reach -40°C.

The meteorologist was keen that the thermometer had both Celsius and Kelvin scales, but this was not a deal breaker for them. They were adamant, however, that they did not want to use a mercury thermometer.

Aside from any concerns about the toxicity of mercury were the thermometer to crack, why might this be the case?

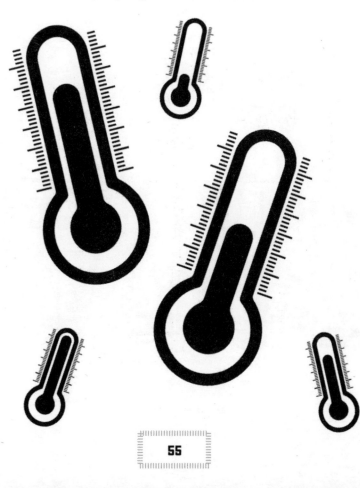

DRIP FEEDING 2

A chemist set up another row of flasks so that she might once again examine the relative corrosiveness of an acid at different concentrations.

Each flask in the row had the same volume of acid poured into it, and then the chemist diluted the acids by adding different volumes of distilled water to each flask.

Working in order along the row, the chemist added one drop of water to the first flask, two drops of water to the second flask, three to the third flask, and so on.

Into which flask would she drop the 50th drop of water?

CUBISM

A geologist wanted to cut a cube of marble into 27 smaller cubes. For this difficult task, there is a specialist piece of cutting equipment which cuts straight slices through the marble at any angle.

a. What is the smallest number of straight cuts through the marble which the geologist would need to make to achieve this, if they are not allowed to rearrange the pieces after each cut?

b. Would the geologist be able to reduce the number of cuts if they *were* able to rearrange the resulting pieces after each cut?

c. If any shape was required, not just a cube, could they reduce the number of cuts needed to make 27 smaller pieces?

DRONING ON

Two meteorologists, a supervisor and their student, are flying a prototype drone over a flat landscape in attempt to observe the after-effects of some adverse weather.

They take turns flying the drone away from them and then back, using a straight, unbending flight path in both directions. In particular, the supervisor flies the first leg of the outbound journey, and then the student takes over for the final 500m. When the drone reaches its maximum distance from them, the pilots swap again so that the supervisor flies the drone for the first 300m back, and then the student completes the journey.

Which of the pair flew the drone for the greater distance? How much farther did they fly it?

THE CAKE IS A LIE

One day, Einstein found himself in a university canteen. At the table next to his he observed a group of researchers who were discussing their various findings in each of the latest experiments into the possibility of dimensional portals.

Einstein further observed that at the table were three supervisors and three students, who had each eaten exactly one slice of cake during their discussion. But he also observed, however, a seemingly contradictory fact that a total of only four slices of cake had been eaten by them.

How is this possible?

ROCK, PAPER, MINERAL

A geologist was examining the mineral makeup of a sample of marble for data which was due to be published in an upcoming research paper that they were working on.

They had identified five distinct minerals in the sample, all of which were present in different quantities:

- There was less silica in the sample than dolomite

- Alumina was the least prevalent

- Serpentine was the third-most prevalent mineral

- There was more calcite in the sample than silica

- Dolomite was not the most prevalent

Can you order the five minerals in the sample from most to least prevalent?

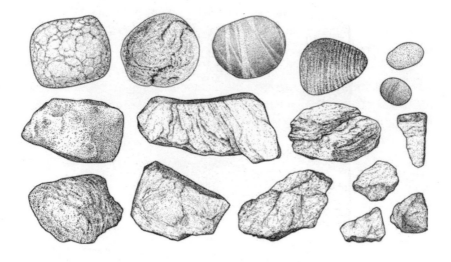

A ROCK AND A HARD PLACE

A professor and her student had been working in a lab to create manufactured jewels. They were pleased with their work to date, since it had resulted in ten lab-grown diamonds.

As a thank you for his hard work, the professor allowed her student an opportunity to keep one of the lab-made diamonds for himself.

She produced two opaque bags, marked to make clear that:

- One of the bags had the ten diamonds in it

- The other bag had ten fake gems which were indistinguishable by touch from the set of diamonds

The professor said that her student could—while blindfolded—choose a bag at random. Whichever bag he touched first, he could then pull one stone from the chosen bag. If it was one of the lab-grown diamonds, he could keep it.

To give him more than a 50:50 chance, the student was allowed to rearrange the gems between the bags however he chose before the blindfold was applied. However, once the blindfold was applied the bags were moved around—without rearranging the diamonds—so he would not know which bag was which.

How could the student rearrange the diamonds and gems between the two bags to give himself the highest possible chance of choosing a diamond when he picked a bag at random?

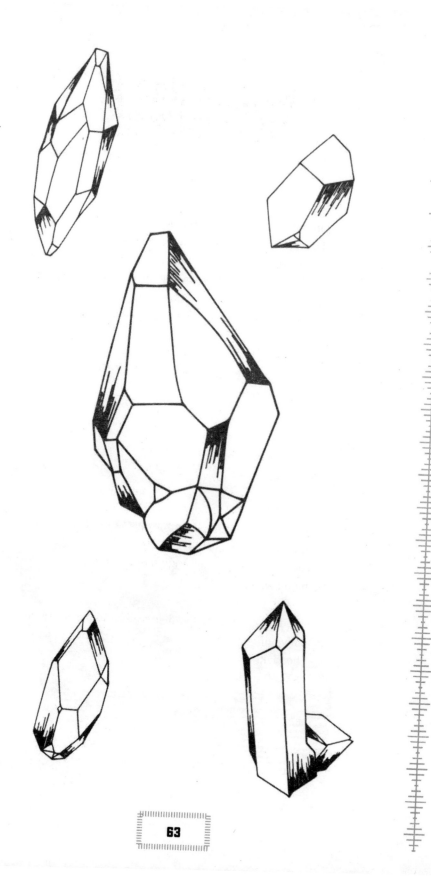

UPSIDE DOWN

A colleague of Einstein's, who had been particularly intrigued by his theory describing how light would bend through space, was demonstrating the effect of a curved lens on images. In particular, she wanted to show how some lenses were able to invert an image, so that it appeared upside-down.

On her desk, she had placed not only the inverting lens but also:

- A small Norwegian flag

- A postcard of the Eiffel Tower

- A deck of cards, from which she had randomly selected the eight of diamonds.

Which of the three would be the most useful in demonstrating to her students the inverting effect of a lens?

DOING IT BY HALVES

The half-lives of five new radioactive isotopes were being compared in a secure facility where Einstein sometimes worked.

As yet unnamed, the five isotopes had each been given a code name for the duration of the experiment.

The findings were as follows:

- Victor's half-life was longer than Papa's

- Yankee's half-life was longer than Tango's, but not the longest overall

- Tango did not have the shortest half-life

- Lima's half-life was shorter than Victor's

Which isotope had the longest half-life?

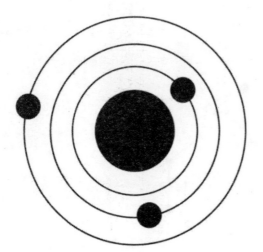

CONSTELLATION CONUNDRUM

An astronomer working alongside Einstein was examining images of a recently discovered star cluster, which demonstrated remarkable symmetry in its arrangement of stars.

When describing the cluster to his colleagues, he noted that the ten stars were arranged in such a way as to form five straight lines, with four stars in each line.

How could this be possible?

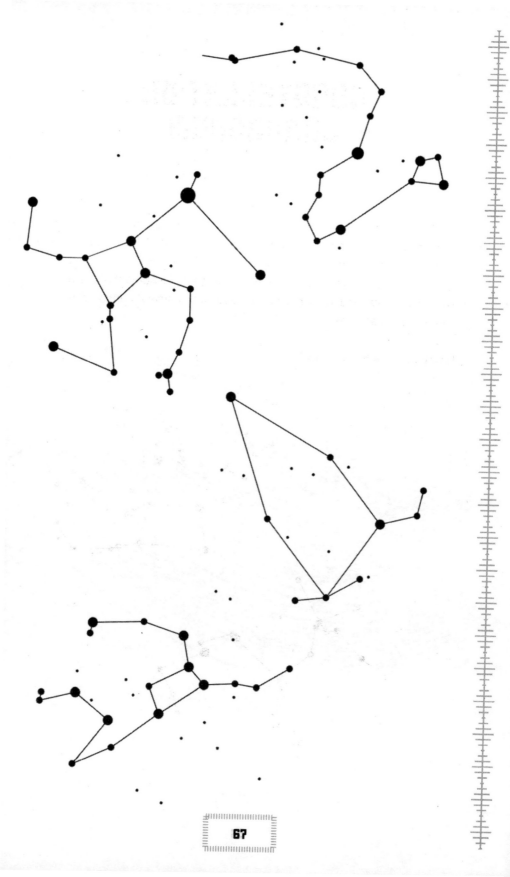

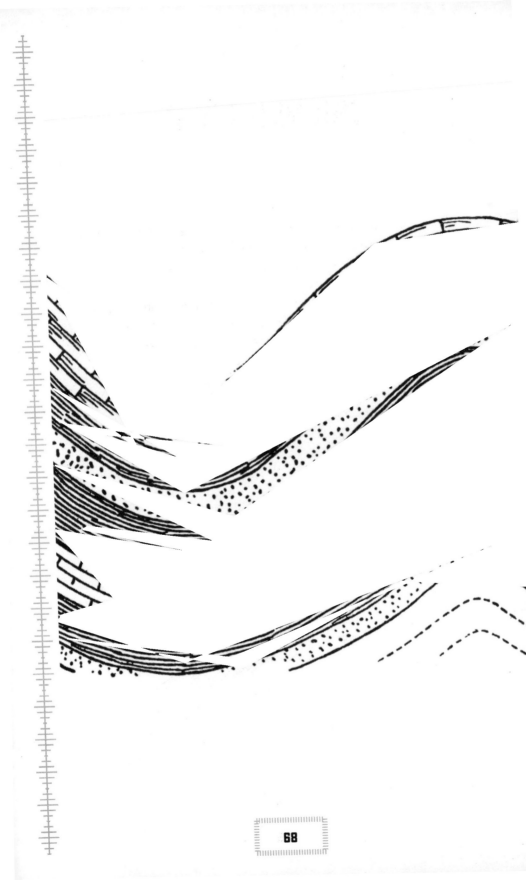

CAN YOU DIG IT

Two geologists were standing above the edge of a large trench which had been dug the previous day, and which they planned to use to examine the mineral content of the soft earth found in the local area.

While leaning in to get a closer look at the trench, one of the geologists fell in. It was too deep for them to be able to climb out, and the only object they could find within the trench was a small shovel.

The one still above trench said to the other, "I don't have anything to pull you out with, but you don't need me—you can use the shovel."

The other replied, "But I can't stand on it, and it won't take my weight—and there's nowhere to tunnel out to!"

But the geologist outside the trench insisted that it was easily done.

How could the unfortunate geologist use the shovel to get themselves out of the hole?

TWO BY TWO

A friend of Einstein's wished to take some pictures of a solar eclipse, which he hoped might prove themselves of some scientific value. For this purpose, however, the eclipse was to be best viewed from a certain island archipelago in the southern hemisphere.

In fact, due to the remoteness of the island they wished to take the photographs from, the researcher needed to use six different local ferries to reach the site.

The local ferries did not have set prices, and instead simply asked passengers to pay half the number of dollars that they were carrying at the time they boarded. As a gesture of goodwill, they would then give a dollar back when they left the ferry.

How many dollars should the astronomer carry before boarding the first ferry, in order to spend the least amount of money?

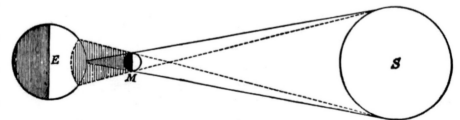

SMASHING STUFF

Two technicians were each carrying a box of test tubes to one of Einstein's laboratories, with thirty test tubes in each of their boxes.

When the technicians reached the lab, however, each of them realized that some of the test tubes had smashed in the box they were carrying.

"Over half of mine are smashed," complained one technician, counting them out.

"Ah, I have exactly as many broken test tubes in my box as you have unbroken test tubes in yours," replied the other.

How many test tubes remained unbroken?

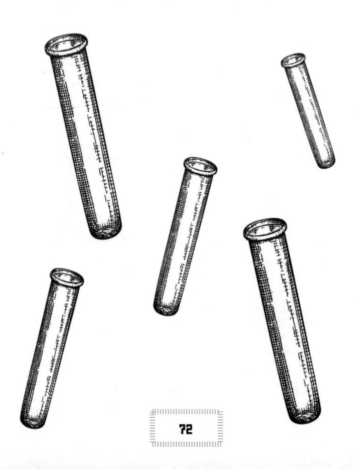

POUR PERFORMANCE

A lab technician needed to measure out exactly 500ml of an alkaline solution that was to be used as part of a chemistry experiment.

The lab had an effectively unlimited supply of the alkaline solution, but due to an accident that had destroyed an entire cupboard full of equipment it held limited measuring equipment.

The only measuring items that were still functional were two flasks, one of which would hold exactly 300ml when full, and the other one of which would hold exactly 700ml when full.

If we assume the technician can pour away any unneeded solution, how can they measure out exactly the 500ml required for the experiment?

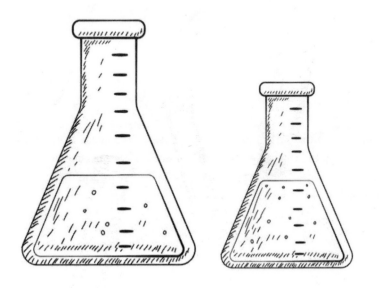

TIME TO REFLECT 1

An astronomer was taking several detailed photographs of a galaxy at night, which had previously been difficult to capture on film.

When he developed the film, he was intrigued to find the result shown below:

After capturing the galaxy on several occasions, however, the astronomer noted that an error in their development process was causing the images of the galaxy to be reflected when the final photograph was produced.

Which of the options, "a" to "d" below, is a true reflection of the image opposite, if the shaded line represents the mirror in which the image should be reflected?

a.

b.

c.

d.

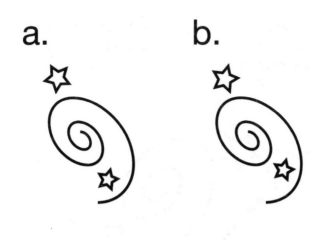

CHEMISTRY COMPARISON

Two chemists have been tasked with tidying up a pile of containers in a lab, each of which contains a sample of a particular chemical element.

- A third of the containers hold gaseous elements

- Twelve of the containers hold solid elements

- If they were to divide the containers holding liquid elements evenly, each chemist would get one liquid element container each

How many containers are there in total?

TEAM TALK

Two researchers were discussing how many people would be working with them on an upcoming experiment that they had designed, which was based on a thought experiment Einstein had discussed years earlier.

One of the researchers noted that they would have twice as many female colleagues in the team as male colleagues.

The second researcher noted that they would have the same number of male colleagues as female colleagues.

Assuming that both researchers were speaking accurately about the same cohort of people, could they both be correct? If so, how many additional people would be working with the two researchers?

SHARE IT OUT

A geology professor brought a briefcase containing exactly ten rock samples to a lab for testing.

There were ten scientists in the lab, and each of them was due to test one of the samples to determine its mineral structure. After a week, they would report their findings.

When the professor had given out all of the rock samples equally between the ten scientists, however, there was still exactly one sample left in the briefcase. How is this possible?

CIRCULAR DEFINITION

A biologist set up an arrangement of Petri dishes in a circle, each with a different culture of microorganisms growing within it.

Moving around the circle of dishes in a clockwise direction, he marked the first dish "1," the second dish "2," the third dish "3," and so on until he had numbered them all. The dishes were all equally spaced around the circle.

After three days, the biologist noticed similar activity occurring in the 8th and 32nd petri dishes. This was particularly striking as the two dishes were directly opposite one another in the circle.

How many Petri dishes were there in total?

SHINE BRIGHT

An engineer was comparing the relative brightness of two lightbulbs. The lightbulbs had been designated as Alpha and Beta, and their brightnesses were measured in lumens.

- Between them, the two bulbs produced 1,000 lumens.

- Alpha, however, produced 60 more lumens than Beta.

What was the output, in lumens, of each lightbulb?

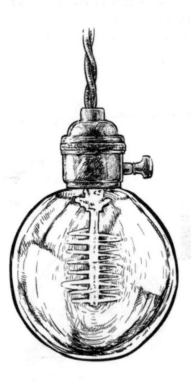

STATISTICALLY SPEAKING

Einstein was visiting a friend at a nearby university, who was a mathematics professor. The professor told his friend about a most unusual situation which had occurred at the end of a long academic year.

After a final statistics examination, the professor had asked each of the students in turn how many of the questions they were able to attempt on the paper. None of the students were aware of the responses of their classmates.

To the professor's surprise, he calculated that three-quarters of the students believed that they had answered an above-average number of questions for an examination of that type.

The professor presented this finding to his students, and asked if it was possible for 75% of the students to have answered an above-average number of questions.

Is it possible? The average being used is the mean.

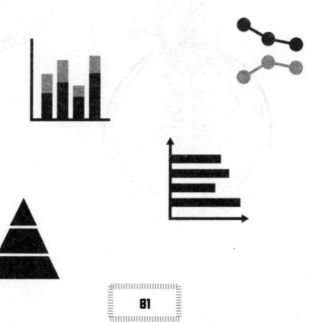

HEADS UP

While studying the various chemical compounds present in a set of coins, a metallurgist working in Einstein's research facility accidentally fused two different coins together. The resulting hybrid coin had the head of one coin on one side and the tail of the other coin on the other, but because the coins were made of different materials it was heavily biased to land on one side more than the other when flipped.

After Einstein came in to suggest a break, the pair decided to flip the coin to decide which of two lunch spots to visit.

In doing so, they came up with a way of flipping the biased coin so that it gave them the same equal odds as a non-weighted coin would.

How could they do it?

THE VETERAN

A geologist was comparing sedimentary rock samples taken early in his career with more recently sourced ones.

While each rock had been formed many millions of years ago, he had marked each rock with the date the sample was extracted.

Looking in particular at two samples, A and B, he noted that:

- When he wrote a paper about the two samples six years previously, sample A had been gathered two-and-half times as many years ago as sample B

- Today, however, sample A had been gathered only twice as long ago as sample B

How many years ago had each sample been gathered?

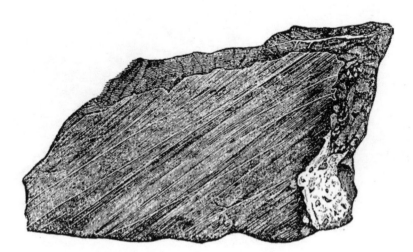

ADD AND MULTIPLY

An aeronautical agency calculated that, in just the last three years, they had sent six astronauts in total into space.

One of the members of the team noticed that adding up the numbers of astronauts sent in each of the three years—that is, the number sent in year 1 plus the number sent in year 2 plus the number sent in year 3— would give the same total as if these three numbers had been multiplied together instead.

If each year they sent the same number or fewer astronauts than the year before, how many astronauts did they send in each year?

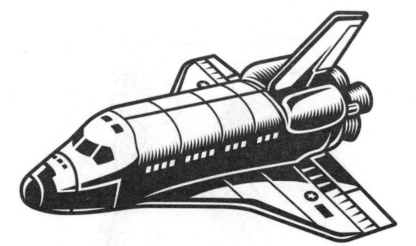

THE MIX-UP

One of the many labs at the university where Einstein worked was currently home to several visually identical vials of clear liquid. Some held acid, while others held alkali.

The vials were being stored in a cupboard with three shelves in it. One shelf had only acid vials placed on it, one shelf had only alkali vials, and the third shelf had both acid and alkali vials on it.

Each shelf had been given a label, with one each of "ACID," "ALKALI," and "ACID OR ALKALI".

It transpired, however, that whoever placed the labels on the shelves had muddled them up, so that all of the shelves had the wrong label on.

How could someone use a single litmus test, on a vial from just one of the shelves, to determine which shelf has which liquids on it?

THE LOSING LECTURER

During a long break between lectures, Einstein and two of his colleagues decided to have a speed chess tournament. As there were three of them, they decided that the winner of each game should stay on each time and play the loser of the previous game.

The three lecturers were each from different fields. Between them there was one each from the fields of biology, chemistry, and physics—which was Einstein.

From a total of eleven games, Einstein won a total of five.

Did Einstein play in the first match?

THE UNKNOWABLE CUBE 1

Two astronomers were busy discussing the dark side of the moon, when the topic of conversation turned to a debate about whether or not its appearance can be inferred by what can be observed in those areas of space around it.

As a thought experiment, one of the astronomers designed a scheme for the other whereby they would show them a hypothetical cubic planet from various angles, and have them determine what should appear on an unadorned face of the cube.

Here is the test they designed:

Can you say which of these five faces below should appear on the cube in place of the blank face, ignoring rotation?

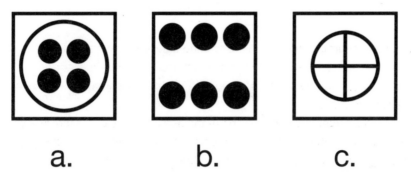

a.

b.

c.

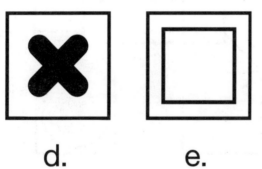

d.

e.

A chemist had written out the following digits on her desk:

When a colleague entered the room, she demonstrated how a single item from her desk could simultaneously turn the numbers above into the elements boron, hydrogen, iodine, and oxygen. The item was not a pen or other writing implement.

What item did she use to bring about the change?

INSTITUTIONAL INDICATOR

Two scientific institutes had joined together to create a research project which was due to last for several years.

The two institutes, one of which was delighted to have Einstein speak at its opening ceremony, had been founded in different years. The head of the new project commented that the project's duration in years would be exactly equal to the current age of the most recently founded institute.

A colleague then noted that the combined age of the two institutions was equal to the first square number, counting up from 1, whose first and third digits were identical. The project lead then acknowledged that, while this was true, one of the colleges was ten times the age of the other.

How long would the joint research project last?

THE LOST BRIEFCASES

Three professors were all in the lost property office at their university, having misplaced their briefcases. Each academic belonged to a different branch of the chemistry department, but had left their briefcases in different locations across the university. Fortunately, all three had been handed in.

All of their briefcases were visually indistinguishable from the outside, so they were each required to identify one scientific item that could be found inside their case, in order to positively identify it as theirs.

- The briefcase with the test tube did not belong to the analytical chemist

- A briefcase was found in the modern languages department

- The biochemist's briefcase was left in the cafeteria

- The conical flask was in the inorganic chemist's briefcase

- The briefcase left in the library contained a microscope

Which scientist left which briefcase where?

THE DOCTORAL PAPERS

Three doctoral candidates had all submitted their theses on the same day. All three had done so by an agreed deadline of noon, although they handed their manuscripts over at different times. Each candidate specialized in a different area of physics, and each had chosen to dedicate their thesis to a practitioner who had particularly influenced them.

- The optics thesis was not the one dedicated to Planck

- The thesis dedicated to Schrödinger was neither first nor last to be handed in

- The thermodynamics thesis was handed in last

- The thesis specializing in quantum mechanics was dedicated to Bohr

Now answer the following questions:

1. Which was the first thesis to be handed in, and to whom was it dedicated?

2. To whom was the thermodynamics thesis dedicated?

A lab technician was looking at the relative weights of beakers and test tubes used in a lab. Using a balance scale, she observed that all of the test tubes were identical in weight to one another, and all of the beakers were identical in weight to one another.

She then placed six test tubes on the left side of the scale, and a single test tube on the right side of the scale. To the right side she then added a beaker, which she knew weighed 100g.

The scales balanced, so how much did one test tube weigh?

TEMPERATURE
EXPERIMENT 1

A set of thermometers has been carefully arranged to fill a square tray, as shown opposite. Each was set to measure the temperature of a particular substance, and the results were collated by writing various numbers outside the tray. The mercury was then drained out of each thermometer.

Can you shade in some or all of each thermometer to show the level the mercury reached in each thermometer during the experiment? Each number outside the tray shows the total number of grid squares in that row or column which should contain mercury. Each grid square is either entirely filled with mercury or entirely empty, and each thermometer must be filled from the bulb outward.

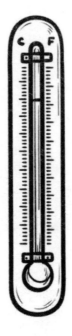

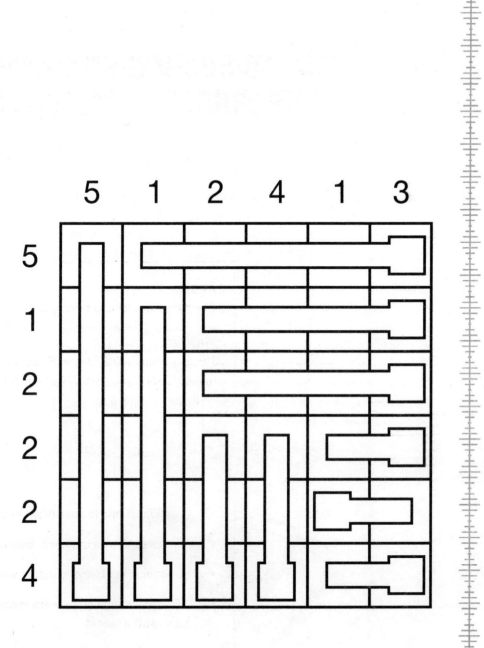

IT TAKES TWO
TO MANGO

A biologist had sliced up several mangoes before beginning an experiment into their fermentation levels under specific conditions.

The mangoes needed to be pulped before testing, so the biologist had peeled and chopped the fruit, and then added all of the flesh into a single container.

Before beginning the experimental method, however, the biologist realized that they had not made a note of how many individual mangoes had been used. Due to the varying sizes of the fruit, it could not be accurately deduced from the total weight of the mango flesh.

Einstein, who happened to be passing by the open door of the lab as this conundrum was being considered, was able to suggest an easy way for the researcher to find out the number of individual fruits which had been included in the experiment.

What do you think his suggestion was?

A chemist was heating up a certain solution in a beaker, when it reacted in such a way as to obscure the measurement markings on the side of the glass.

Before the experiment had begun the cylindrical beaker had been just over half full, and it was clear that some of the liquid had evaporated since.

Without pouring any liquid out, or using another measuring device, how could the chemist discover whether the beaker was still more than half full?

COMPOSITE IMAGE 1

After taking several high-definition photographs over the course of several months, a team of astronomers attempted to create a composite image of a star cluster in a distant galaxy. In the final stages, the team produced a stylized mock-up of the cluster image to make sure that individual stars were all correctly aligned.

The two images opposite are the final pieces which must be merged to create the complete composite picture.

If the two images are overlaid so that the two areas of detail on one image fill in the corresponding blank spaces on the other, how many six-pointed stars would be visible in the composite image?

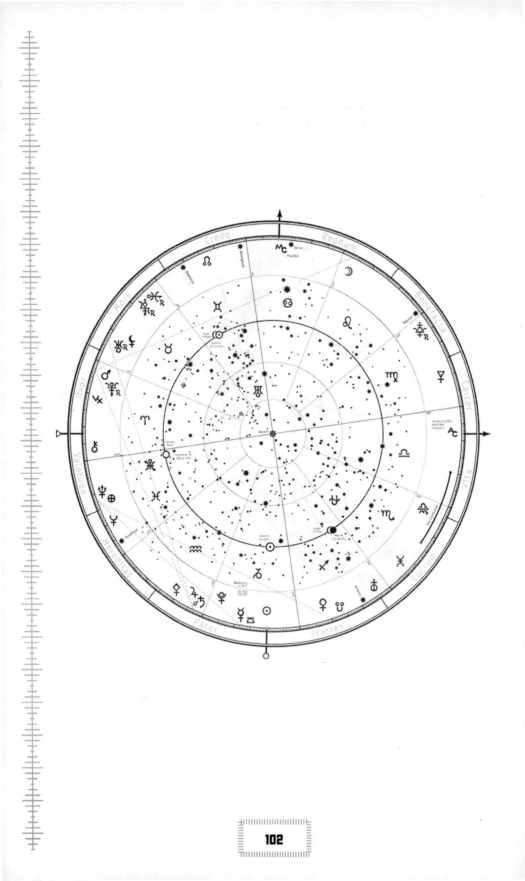

ASTRONOMICAL ODDS

At an astronomical convention given in Einstein's recognition, a group of five outstanding cosmologists were invited to name individual stars in a cluster which they had all jointly discovered.

The cosmologists had not all made equal contributions to the research, so they were invited to name stars in a particular order:

- The first cosmologist named half of the stars in the cluster, plus an extra one

- The next cosmologist named seven of the remaining stars

- The third cosmologist named two-fifths of the remaining stars, plus an extra one

- Next, the fourth cosmologist named 80% of the remaining stars, plus an extra one

By the time this was done, however, there were no stars left for the fifth cosmologist to name.

How many stars were there in the cluster in total?

THE DOCTORAL DUO

An astrophysicist was chatting about the relative merits of two of her doctoral students with Einstein, who was familiar with both of the students.

The students, Ava and Ben, had been studying for the same amount of time at this particular institution, having both begun their PhDs five years ago.

The astrophysicist noted that Ben was now half of Ava's current age. The year before starting his PhD, Ben had been three-sevenths of the age Ava was when she began her PhD. They also observed that the two candidates shared the same birthday.

How old were Ava and Ben, respectively?

STAR SLIDES 1

An astrophysicist had taken several photos of the night sky, each showing a different arrangement of stars and planets within a small area.

She had marked each image with a code, which was determined by the appearance of the celestial objects shown. The final image, however, had not yet been given a code.

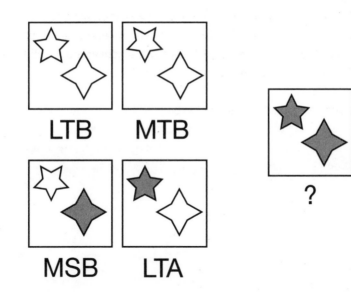

Which of the following five options should replace the question mark?

 a. MSA

 b. LSB

 c. SBT

 d. LSA

 e. MTA

OFFICIAL SECRETS 1

Two national security services were communicating about the possibility of creating a joint nuclear power facility on their shared border. Once the final plans were drawn up, the two head engineers—one from each country, A and B—were particularly keen that the details did not fall into outsider hands.

They decided to send the documents to one another in a special security case, with nation A's engineer sending their version of the final plans to nation B's engineer for approval. Each engineer had a special padlock for the case that only they knew the code for—and which they refused to tell anyone, under any circumstances.

Assuming that the cases could not be opened without unlocking a padlock, how could the two engineers send and receive the documents while using their padlocks for security, without revealing their secret combinations to anyone?

THE LONG AND SHORT OF IT

An astronaut was being fitted one evening for a space suit, which he would wear for a mission to visit a manned space station in outer space. The suit was designed so that it would fit him as precisely as possible for space walks, in order to provide the maximum protection.

After two weeks on the space station, however, the astronaut complained that the suit did not seem to be big enough each time he put it on. In particular, it appeared not to be sufficiently tall to accommodate his height.

Assuming that the astronaut is not a child who was naturally growing taller, why might this be?

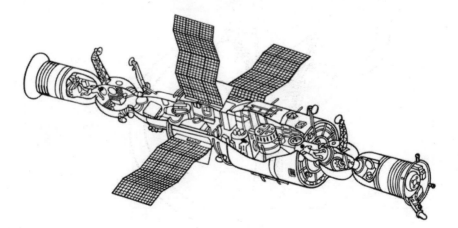

CONFOUNDING COMPOUNDS 1

Can you join all of the atoms below into pairs, so that each pair contains exactly one nitrogen atom, white atoms, and one oxygen atom, shaded atoms, to create the chemical compound nitrogen monoxide?

Join each pair with a straight horizontal or vertical line to show the covalent bond between the pair of elements. Bonds cannot cross over either one another or another atom.

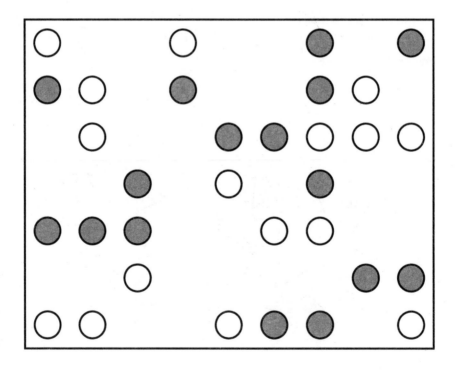

RELATIVE BRILLIANCE

A research group created a series of graphics to provide a visual representation of the luminance of different stars within a single cluster.

In one of these clusters there were eight stars in total in the group. The stars were drawn so that the star's size was directly proportional to its brilliance, as viewed from earth.

Which two of these stars have the same brilliance?

THE ACADEMIC LUNCH

Three professors were sitting in a university cafeteria discussing their latest work. Each belonged to a different discipline, and was visiting on sabbatical from a different academic institution to each of the other two professors. They all drank something different during their discussion.

- The molecular biologist drank lime cordial

- The academic visiting from the University of Tokyo was a chemical engineer

- The person drinking orange cordial was visiting from Oxford University

- The quantum theorist was not the one drinking tea

- One of the academics was visiting from Princeton University

Now answer the following questions:

1. What was the quantum theorist drinking?

2. From which university was the tea-drinker visiting?

3. The professor from Princeton was a specialist in which scientific field?

A SIGN OF WIND

Einstein arrived via train at a large and sprawling research facility, at which he was due to attend a lecture on solar wind. When he arrived on site, he saw a signpost that pointed him in the direction of a building where he could go to sign in, to a lecture hall he needed to later visit, and back to the station he had come from.

Having registered his attendance by signing in, he set out to find the lecture hall but somehow found himself back at the signpost he had originally used on entering the site. Unfortunately, it seemed that since he had used it previously it had been blown over by a strong gust of wind—albeit not a solar one, he chuckled to himself.

The signpost had spun around as it fell, so no longer pointed to the lecture hall he wished to visit. What's more, the arm that had pointed to the sign-in facility had snapped off.

How could he discover the correct way to the venue?

SET THEORY 2

A physicist has sketched the following three groupings in her notebook:

Set A
Beryllium (Be, 4)
Fluorine (F, 9)

Set B
Oxygen (O, 8)
Cobalt (Co, 27)

Set A + B
Hydrogen (H, 1)
Gadolinium (Gd, 64)

Can you work out what classification rules she might have used for each of the sets, in order to sort the compounds in this way? Each element's symbol and atomic number are given for reference.

TAKE YOUR SEATS

Twenty mathematical students of Einstein were attending a short lecture on probability.

The lecture room had capacity for exactly twenty people, and seats were numbered from 1 to 20 accordingly. The attendees had been sent tickets with a number on, indicating which seat they should take.

Before the lecture even began, however, a question of probability is presented to them quite by accident. The first mathematician in the line has lost their numbered ticket, and decides to take a seat at random. The following attendees enter one by one, and sit down one after another. They choose their seats according to the following rule: If their numbered seat is not taken, they will sit in it—otherwise they will choose a seat at random.

What is the probability that the last person in the line sits in their originally assigned seat, if all of the mathematicians follow this rule?

DOUBLE DISCOVERY

A cosmologist who was taking detailed images of the universe discovered evidence of two important exoplanets in the same night, both of which were in the goldilocks zone that theoretically might enable them able to support extraterrestrial life. The discoveries were made an hour apart, with one at 23:30 and the other at half past midnight.

To commemorate the magnitude of the discoveries, the cosmologist's work was celebrated on two different days: one on the date and time of the first discovery, and one on the date and time of the second discovery. A decade after the ground-breaking work, however, the gap between the celebrations of the two discoveries had increased from one to twenty-five hours.

Why might such a gap in time have opened up between the exact anniversaries of the two discoveries?

ROBOT RACE

Two engineers had each built a solar-powered robot, and wanted to race them against one another.

The engineers set up a course on a smooth, straight walkway outside of their research building, which measured 50m from start to finish. One of the robots completed the course in 54 seconds, which was 90% of the time taken by the slower robot.

So confident was the engineer who created the faster robot that she suggested that, even with a head start for the losing robot, her robot could win the race again. To test this, they repositioned the winning robot at the original start line, so it had to complete the 50m course again, but gave the losing robot a 4m head start—so it had to cover only 46m.

Assuming the two robots maintained a constant pace in both races, would the winning robot from the first race still win the second race?

CONFOUNDING COMPOUNDS 2

Can you join all of the atoms below into pairs, so that each pair contains exactly one hydrogen atom, white atoms, and one fluorine atom, shaded atoms, to create the chemical compound hydrogen fluoride?

Join each pair with a straight horizontal or vertical line to show the covalent bond between the pair of elements. Bonds cannot cross over either one another or another atom.

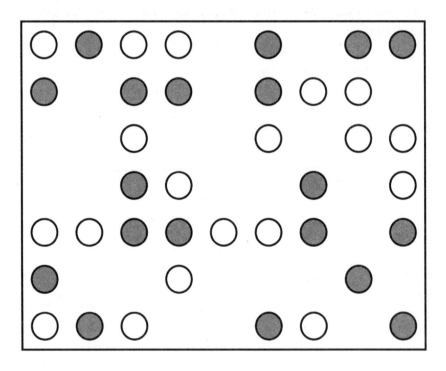

RULE WITH A ROD OF IRON

A metallurgist has two iron rods on his desk, which are visually indistinguishable from one another. One of them has been magnetized, while the other has not.

The two rods lie touching tips on his desk, pulled together by the magnetic attraction.

The metallurgist separates the two bars again.

How can he establish—without using any other items—which rod is the magnetized one?

PEAK BEAKER

A group of one hundred researchers attending a symposium on relativity decided to conduct a casual experiment during a downtime period.

Lined up on a table were one hundred beakers, all upside down. Then one researcher went along the line and turned over every beaker, so that each was the right way up. The second researcher then went along and turned over every other beaker, so that it was upside down again—that is, they turned over beakers 2, 4, 6, 8, and so on. The third researcher turned over every third beaker—so beakers 3, 6, 9, and so on—and then this continued following the same pattern until the 100th researcher went along the line and turned over just the 100th beaker.

How many of the beakers would be the right way up after all one hundred researchers had gone along the line as described above?

TIME TO REFLECT 2

A quantum physicist, studying the apparent bending of light, was looking at several photos of a star cluster which had been taken at different points in time:

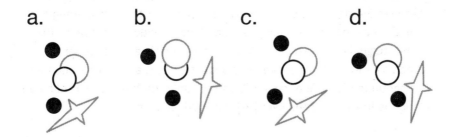

a.   b.   c.   d.

A fifth photograph in the set appeared, however, to be an exact reflection of one of the images ("a" to "d"), as though a mirror had been placed at the angle shown by the dashed line below:

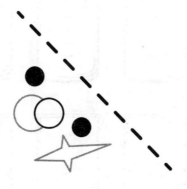

Which of the images, "a" to "d," was it a reflection of?

THE UNFORTUNATE PARTY

A group of physicists working on a fluid dynamics project threw a summer party to celebrate the end of a previous research project. Various drinks and plates of food were shared out among the partygoers, and a large dispensing container of iced water was set up to keep the team hydrated.

The following day, several of the physicists became unwell with an unpleasant virus. Only one item had been consumed by all of the poorly physicists: the water. Strangely, it had also been consumed by a small number of the partygoers who did not become ill.

If all that was in the container was ice and distilled water—and everyone at the party had had at least one glass of it—then how might some of the scientists have escaped illness where others did not? Assume that all of the physicists had the same level of immunity to the virus, and that the container was not refilled at any point during the evening. Assume also that it was not infected by anyone attending the party.

THE COMPOUND EXPERIMENT

Can you complete the missing elements in the "Results" section below?

Abstract
The molecular structure of three different liquids was examined.

Method
Three unidentified acids were examined to determine their atomic makeup. Each liquid was given a code name for the duration of the testing.

Variables
Acid code names: Iota; Zeta; Psi

Observations

- Psi was found to have more hydrogen atoms than Iota

- Iota's structure matched with sulfuric acid

- Zeta was not found to match with the formula for acetic acid

- The following liquids were identified: acetic acid, ethanol, and sulfuric acid

- The compound with the fewest oxygen atoms in its formula had the code name Zeta

- Liquids with the following chemical formulae were identified:

  $C_2H_4O_2$; C_2H_6O; H_2SO_4

Results

Liquid code name	Identified liquid	Identified formula

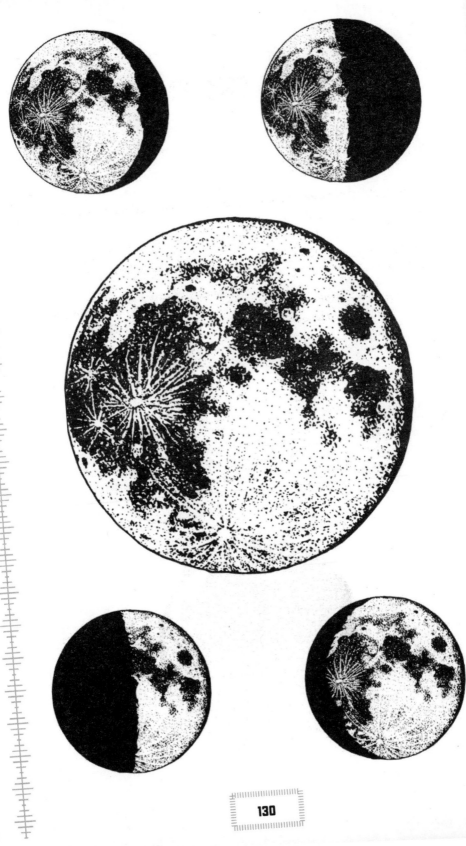

OVER THE MOONS

Three astronomers were comparing photos they had each taken of the same distant planet at different times of the year.

In each photo, a different number of the planet's moons was visible, although all of the moons appeared to be identical in size and appearance.

- Photo A showed the smallest number of moons, with 13 fewer than in Photo B, and a quarter of the number that appeared in Photo C

- When combined, the total number of moons visible in Photos A and C was 45

What is the greatest number of distinct moons that the astronomers could confirm for the planet, based on the photographs they had taken?

MANY MOONS

After discovering an exoplanet in a distant galaxy, a group of astronomers noticed that it was surrounded by several moons. They managed to capture images of each of the ten moons, which they overlaid on top of one another to compare the dimensions of the natural satellites.

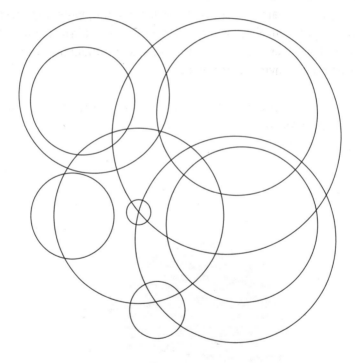

Surprisingly, exactly two of the moons appeared to be the same size. Which two?

TAKING SIDES

After much discussion about the possible faces on a hypothetical cubic planet, the two researchers decided to retire their speculative challenges.

One said to the other, "It's a worthy thought experiment, especially as you can never see all six faces of a cube at once. You have to move either the cube or your head!"

Their fellow researcher replied, however, that they were quite certain that it was in fact entirely possible to see all six faces of an opaque cube without moving either your head or the cube, and without using any mirrors or indeed anything else at all.

How, moving just your eyes but not any other part of your body or the cube, could it be done?

THE UNKNOWABLE CUBE 2

Two researchers were challenging one another to deduce the appearance of the unknown face of a hypothetical cubic planet. As part of the experiment, one researcher was shown four arrangements of the planet, and asked which of a selection must therefore replace a blank cube face.

Can you work out which of the faces, "a" to "e" below, should replace the blank face on the imaginary planet, ignoring rotation?

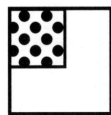

a.

b.

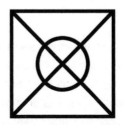

c.

d.

e.

KEEP IT ON FILE

A metallurgist researching various ways of recycling metal waste had two tubs of identical-looking metal filings on his workbench.

He poured the contents of both tubs into a larger container, mixed them up and began to heat them, having assumed that both tubs contained the same metal.

After a while, however, he examined the mixture more carefully and realized that what he actually now had was a mix of both iron and titanium filings. So far no reaction had taken place to the heat, so the researcher set about separating the two sets of filings.

How could the metallurgist separate the mixtures with relative ease?

ON YOUR MARKS

Six academics, who are attempting to review associated papers related to Einstein's theory of relativity, each review a total of six papers each day for six days. Due to the constraints of a specific journal, all of the papers to be read are exactly the same length and take exactly the same amount of time to read.

How many research papers could be read by the six academics in ten days, assuming that each academic continues to read at the same constant rate?

TEMPERATURE EXPERIMENT 2

Another set of thermometers has been carefully arranged to fill a square tray, as shown opposite. Each was set to measure the temperature of a particular substance, and the results were collated by writing various numbers outside the tray. The mercury was then drained out of each thermometer.

Can you shade in some or all of each thermometer to show the level the mercury reached in each thermometer during the experiment? Each number outside the tray shows the total number of grid squares in that row or column which should contain mercury. Each grid square is either entirely filled with mercury or entirely empty, and each thermometer must be filled from the bulb outward.

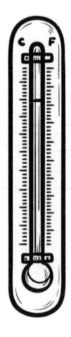

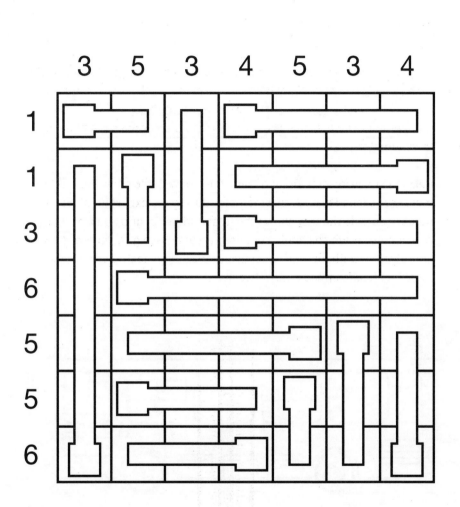

THE SHUTTLE SHUFFLE

Two theoretical physicists at Einstein's university lived on opposite edges of the university campus: one to the far east, and one to the far west.

The campus was served by a shuttle bus which drove from east to west and back again, stopping at the physics department in the middle, where they worked alongside Einstein.

The two physicists happened to each live an equal distance from the physics department, and each was only one stop from the end of the single shuttle bus's route. The route took it back and forth along the same single road that linked right across the compass from west to east/ east to west.

The physicist who lived on the west side observed that whenever he went to stand at the shuttle stop outside of his residence, he first saw the shuttle drive past him on its way westward to the end of the route far more often than he first saw it moving in the direction of the physics department. Meanwhile the east-based physicist proclaimed the opposite: that the shuttle was more often heading to the east end of the line when he went to catch it than in the direction he wished to travel.

How can both claims be true, assuming that their observations are representative samples and not just bad luck?

One of Einstein's students had taken several photos of the night sky, each showing a different arrangement of stars and planets within a small area.

She used a code to identify four of the images, which was determined by the appearance of the celestial objects shown. A fifth image, however, had not yet been assigned a code.

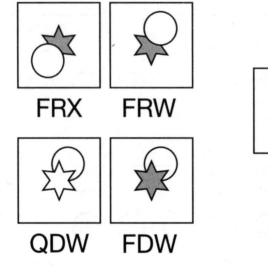

Which of the following codes should replace the question mark symbol?

a. FXW

b. QRX

c. QXW

d. FDX

e. QDX

CONFOUNDING COMPOUNDS 3

Can you join all of the atoms below into pairs, so that each pair contains exactly one silver atom, white atoms, and one iodine atom, shaded atoms, to create the chemical compound silver iodide?

Join each pair with a straight horizontal or vertical line to show the covalent bond between the pair of elements. Bonds cannot cross over either one another or another atom.

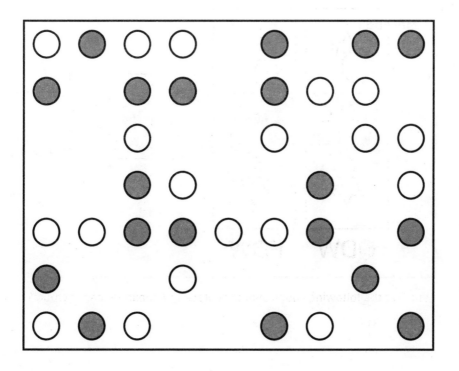

THE BOILING POINTS EXPERIMENT

Can you complete the missing entries in the "Results" section below?

Abstract

The boiling points of three distinct liquid fuels were measured under test conditions.

Method

- Three distinct, clear fuels were tested under controlled conditions to identify their boiling points.

- Three identical beakers were each filled with 100ml of one of the three liquids. All three beakers were heated and their boiling points noted.

- The liquids were given code names and referred to only by these during the experiment.

Variables

Liquid code names: X, Y, and Z

Observations

The three liquids were found to have three different boiling points:

- X's boiling point was measured at 95°C

- One of the boiling points was 72°C

- Z's boiling point was exactly double that of another liquid's

- None of the boiling points was higher than 100°C

- All the boiling points were whole numbers

Results

1. X's boiling point: 95°C

2. Y's boiling point: _____°C

3. Z's boiling point: _____°C

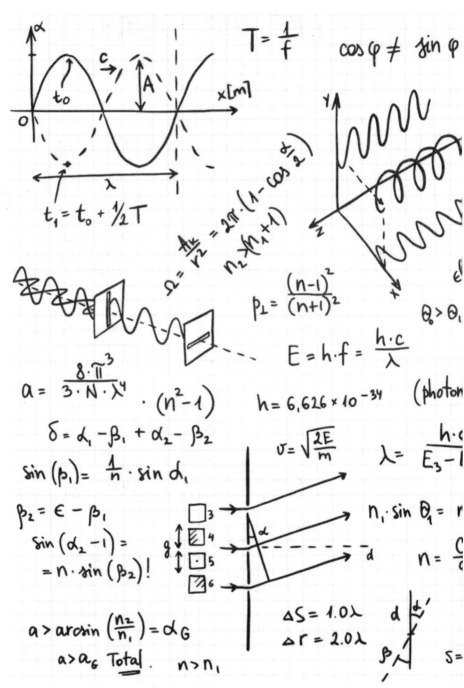

$$T = \frac{1}{f}$$

$$\cos\varphi \neq \sin\varphi$$

$$t_1 = t_0 + \tfrac{1}{2}T$$

$$\Omega = \frac{t_w}{r^2} = 2\pi\cdot\left(1 - \cos\tfrac{\alpha}{2}\right)$$

$$n_2 > (n_1 + 1)$$

$$p_\perp = \frac{(n-1)^2}{(n+1)^2}$$

$$E = h\cdot f = \frac{h\cdot c}{\lambda}$$

$$a = \frac{8\cdot\tilde{\pi}^3}{3\cdot N\cdot\lambda^4}\cdot(n^2-1)$$

$$h = 6{,}626 \times 10^{-34} \quad \text{(photon}$$

$$\delta = \alpha_1 - \beta_1 + \alpha_2 - \beta_2$$

$$\sin(\beta_1) = \frac{1}{n}\cdot\sin\alpha_1$$

$$v = \sqrt{\frac{2E}{m}} \qquad \lambda = \frac{h\cdot c}{E_3 - }$$

$$\beta_2 = \epsilon - \beta_1$$

$$\sin(\alpha_2 - 1) =$$
$$= n\cdot\sin(\beta_2)!$$

$$n_1\cdot\sin\theta_1 =$$

$$n = \frac{c}{}$$

$$\Delta S = 1{,}0\lambda$$
$$\Delta r = 2{,}0\lambda$$

$$a > \arcsin\left(\frac{n_2}{n_1}\right) = \alpha_G$$
$$a > a_G \text{ Total.} \quad n > n_1$$

$$\theta_0 > \theta_1$$

UPS AND DOWNS

Einstein was sat in the common room, idly watching two professors marking mathematics papers. One of the two was complaining about how many of the papers seemed to have been submitted upside-down. In his pile of 42 papers, he counted that only 13 were facing the right way up in his pile.

The second professor set her colleague a challenge as follows: If, without looking, he could create two piles of papers from his pile of 42, in which both piles had the same number of face-up papers, she would mark all of the papers in both piles.

Assuming that the first professor did not remember which paper was which way up in his pile, how could he guarantee sorting them into two piles, each with the same number of face-up papers, if he was not allowed to look at them as he did so?

$= 657 \, nm$

$\sin \theta_2$

c_o Medium

$\dfrac{(45°)}{5} \Rightarrow \beta$

$\times 3mm = 0{,}98 \, mm$

-0.5

$\alpha \uparrow \downarrow$
$\alpha \neq 0.$

$GaAs \quad \lambda \approx 950 \, nm \, (IR) \, , 630 \, (R)$

$n_{gls} \quad n_s \quad n_{air}$

$\dfrac{1}{f} = (n-1) \times$

$\times \left(\dfrac{1}{r_1} + \dfrac{1}{r_2} \right).$

$D = \dfrac{1}{f} = 0{,}42 \, m^{-1}$

TIME FOR CHANGE

A mathematician, who was determined to beat Einstein in a round-robin chess tournament, wanted to buy a copy of a chess magazine that cost exactly one US dollar.

She looked in her purse and saw that she could pay for the magazine with exact change, made up of multiple coins:

- She had exactly one dollar in change

- She had four different values of coin in her purse

- She had a different number of each value of coin

- She didn't have more than five of any value of coin

- Exactly one coin was worth ten cents

What coins did she have in their pocket? US coins less than one dollar are available in values of 1¢, 5¢, 10¢, 25¢, and 50¢.

SET THEORY 3

A science technician has written the following three groupings in her notebook:

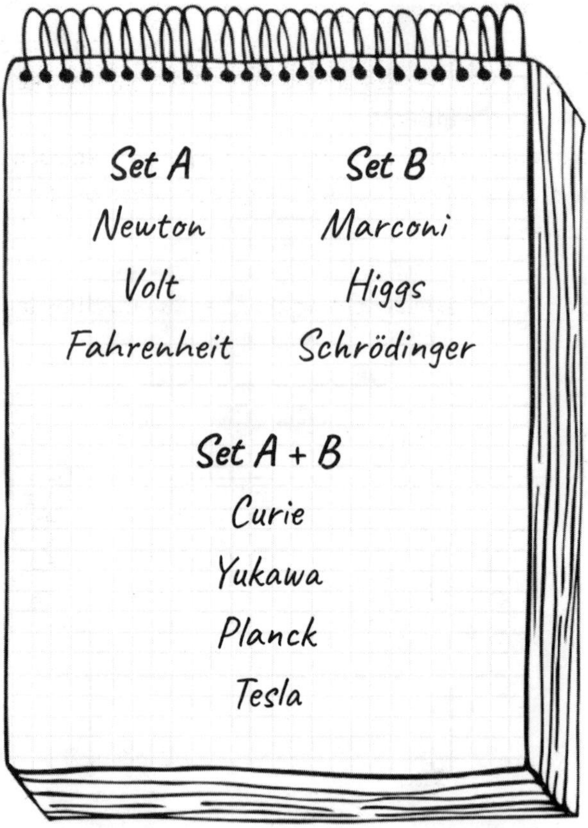

Set A
Newton
Volt
Fahrenheit

Set B
Marconi
Higgs
Schrödinger

Set A + B
Curie
Yukawa
Planck
Tesla

Can you work out what classification rules she might have used for each of the sets, in order to sort the names in this way?

CUMULATIVE CHEMISTRY

A marine biologist is working on a project to create lab-grown corals, with a view to transplanting them into the wild in a year's time.

On the first day of the experiment, he manages to set up one tank, for one new coral to grow in.

On the second day, he sets up a second tank, for a total of two.

On the third day, he sets up two more tanks; then three on the fourth day and five on the fifth day.

The biologist carried on with the same pattern, so each day he set up the same number of new tanks as had been added on the two previous days combined.

On what day of the experiment would he set up the 100th tank?

BY THE BOOK

A doctoral student borrowed two books on the same day from different libraries, one book per library, but then forgot to return them before the deadline.

An astrophysics book—recommended by Einstein—had been borrowed from a library which fined borrowers 1 dollar a day for each day the book was late.

A meteorology book had been borrowed from a library which fined borrowers 5 cents on the first day, but then doubled the outstanding fine every day until the book was returned.

Both books had the same return deadline. Nine days after that deadline, which book had amassed the larger fine?

SUMS OF STEEL

Two engineers were dividing 1m-long rods of steel into shorter rods for future use, cutting them exactly in half so as to form two 50cm-long rods.

One of the engineers commented that they were fortunate to have such accurate tools at their disposal that they could cut so precisely.

The other replied, "But if instead we were to take each rod and cut it into two pieces at a random point along its length, so that it resulted in a smaller piece and a bigger piece, what do you think the average length of the bigger piece would be?"

What is the answer to the question?

THE SOLAR ECLIPSE EXPERIMENT

Can you complete the missing elements in the "Results" section below?

Abstract

The positions of stars were measured during and after a solar eclipse, in an attempt to prove some properties predicted by Einstein's theory of general relativity.

Method

Three telescopes were set up to take regular photographs not only throughout the solar eclipse but also at night following the eclipse. The relative positions of the stars were measured to examine whether the eclipse had altered the apparent position of the stars during the eclipse.

The telescopes were positioned in three different locations across the world.

A dedicated team was positioned at each telescope for the duration of the experiment, and each team was given a code name for ease of reference.

Variables

Observation stations: Brazil; Italy; São Tomé and Príncipe

Weather conditions: Overcast; Clear; Intermittent cloud

Three observation teams: Alpha; Delta; Gamma

Observations

The three observation stations all experienced different weather conditions, which hampered some teams. On the day of the eclipse:

- The team named Delta recorded completely overcast conditions

- Clear skies were recorded in Brazil

- The team in São Tomé and Príncipe observed intermittent cloud

- The Brazilian team was not code-named Alpha

Results

1. The Delta team were positioned in _____

2. The _____ team were positioned in Brazil

3. Intermittent cloud was observed by the _____ team

Two cosmologists were analyzing images they had taken of a distant galaxy, which appeared to feature a black hole:

In the image above, however, they noticed that an issue with the main mirror in their telescope meant that they had received the image upside-down.

Which of the options below, "a" to "d," shows the image that they should have received?

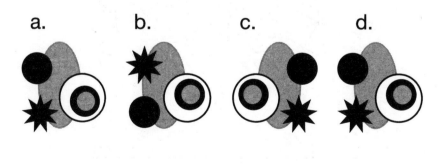

a.	b.	c.	d.

HIDDEN STAR

A cosmologist was studying the development of a supernova star in a nearby galaxy. It usually appeared on their instruments as this seven-pointed star below:

In several of the most recent images she had gathered, however, light interference from other stars made it difficult to spot the supernova in question. Can you find it in the image below, noting that the star may have grown, shrunk, or been rotated compared to the image above?

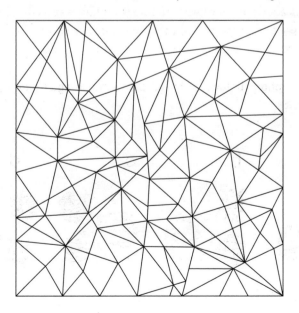

COMPOSITE IMAGE 2

After studying a particular section of the night sky for a month, an astronomer had created a composite image of the distinct celestial bodies which had appeared in the quadrant. In particular, several perfectly circular asteroids had been spotted in the astronomer's field of study.

In these images, shown before the final compositing had occurred, the blank quadrants in one image can be replaced by the detail from the corresponding quadrants in the other image.

If the two images are combined in this way, how many asteroids will be visible, in total, in the completed image?

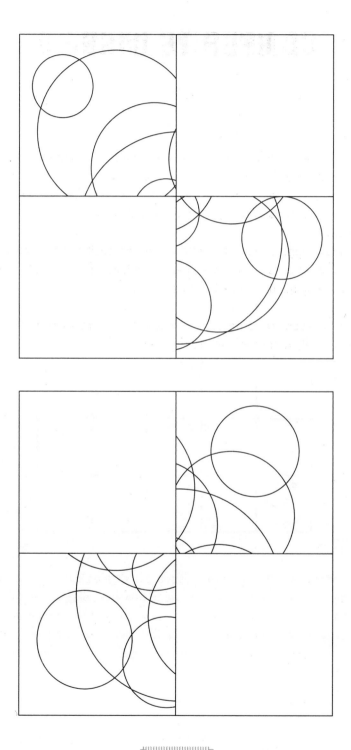

STEP BY STEP

A team of astronauts is directing a rover to explore a hitherto unknown section of Mars.

They have mapped out a square area of the planet, and subdivided it into 25 smaller grid squares:

The rover starts in the bottom-left square, indicated by the hexagon. It can move either up or right—relative to the above diagram—into a touching grid square, but cannot move diagonally. It has no reverse movement. If the rover begins in the bottom-left square, how many possible different routes through the grid squares are there to the top-right square?

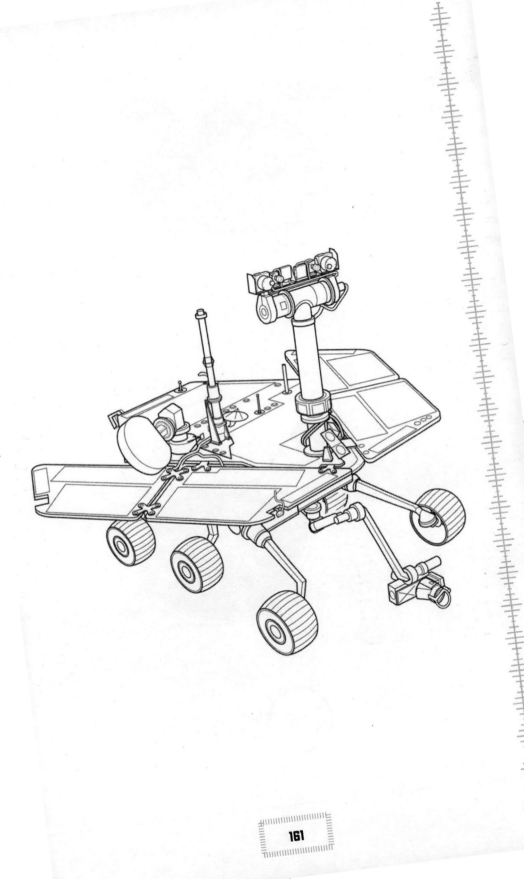

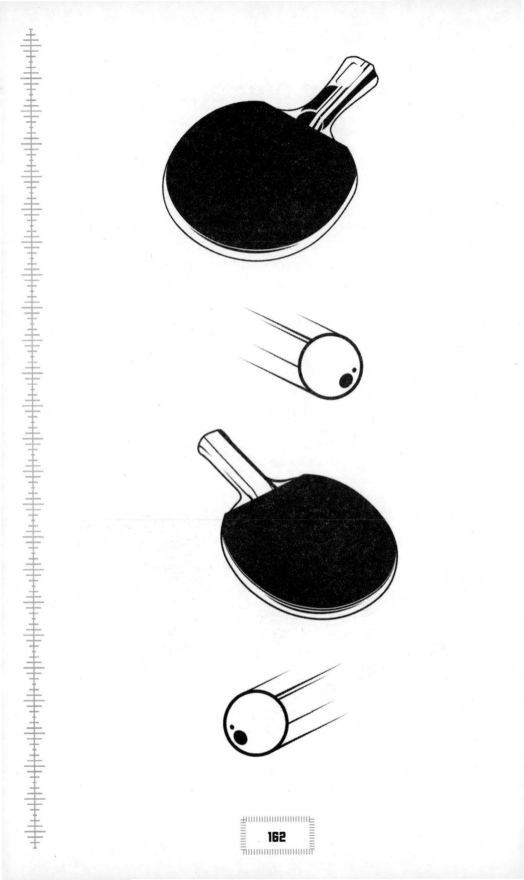

IT'S A REAL KNOCKOUT

In an international research facility, all of the scientists decided to have a knockout ping-pong tournament in their free time. The winner of each game would go on to play the winner of another game, and any losers would be permanently eliminated and unable to play further.

In total, 63 matches were played and every member of the department played in at least one game. There was, eventually, one winner.

How many people were in this particular department, and how many rounds were there in the tournament?

IT'S A HYPOTHETICAL KNOCKOUT

In a break from a symposium at which Einstein was presenting a plenary session, a group of professors were discussing the possible outcomes of a chess tournament that used a standard knockout format. In this particular tournament, one person would be eliminated in each game, and the winner would go on to play the winner of a different game in the previous round.

Before the tournament, all of the players were ranked in ability with a number. A rank of 1 was given to the best player, 2 to the second best, and so on.

In this particular tournament the ranking turned out to be very well chosen, since everyone was beaten by someone with a better ranking than them.

a. For this to be true, which is the earliest round in which the person ranked 2 could be knocked out?

b. What is the greatest difference in rankings that there could be between two players in the final match, if 16 players began the tournament?

OFFICIAL SECRETS 2

Five engineers, all due to work on a space exploration project, were to be entrusted with the key code to a safe that contained top-secret documentation. Inside the safe were the plans for the project which, if they fell into other hands, could be used for nefarious purposes.

To ensure that none of the engineers were given access to the code before it was absolutely necessary, a failsafe was put in place. This meant that each of them knew one fact about the code, although none of them knew the code in its entirety. These five facts were:

- The digits all decreased in value from left to right

- No adjacent digits had a difference of either 2 or 3

- The digits summed to 20

- There were no repeated digits

- The code was an even number

What was the four-digit code?

MIRROR, MIRROR

Two mirrors had been installed in a vertical position at a meteorological station, with each facing in an opposite direction. One faced east, and the other faced west. The mirrors were to be used as part of an experiment to track the sun's movement during an upcoming astronomical event.

Despite facing in different directions, it was noted that when the sun shone on the reflective side of one mirror, it occasionally reflected the sun's light so that it landed on the reflective side of the other mirror. Neither of the mirrors had curved surfaces.

How is this possible, if there are no additional mirrors involved?

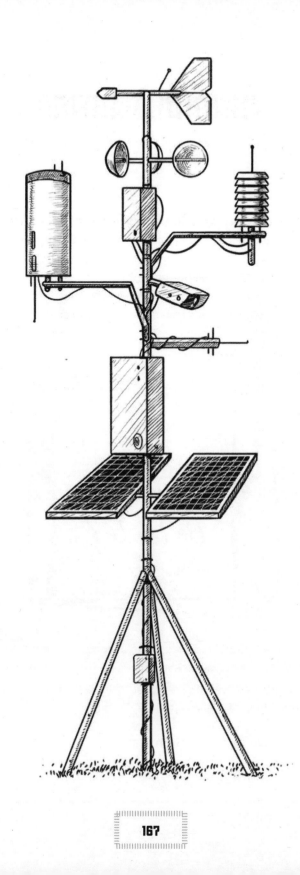

A SHORT NOTE

A researcher was clearing up her workbench after the completion of a project, and found the following note from a colleague:

At first, the note seemed to be a stream of consciousness, committed to paper, from a somewhat erratic colleague. On closer inspection, however, the words began to make more sense. In fact, they had used this list for one of their early experiments.

What did the contents of the note indicate?

An astrophysicist had taken several photos of the night sky, each showing a different arrangement of stars and planets within a small area.

She identified each image with a code, which was determined by the appearance of the celestial objects shown. The final image, however, had not yet been given a code.

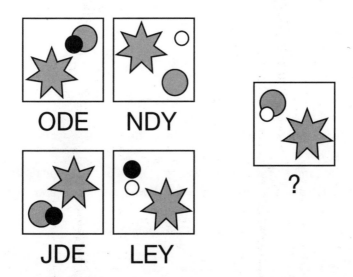

ODE   NDY

JDE   LEY

?

Which of the following options is the only one that can replace the question mark symbol?

- a. JDY
- b. NDE
- c. LDY
- d. ODY
- e. LDE

THE CANDLE WICKING EXPERIMENT

Can you complete the missing elements in the table in the "Results" section below?

Abstract
Three types of wax candle were tested to see how quickly each burned, and to make notes on the capillary action of each wax and wick type.

Method
Three cylindrical candles were used, each formed of a different wax. All three candles were the same height and circumference. Each candle's wick was made from a different material to the other two.

The candles were lit with wooden tapers and the time taken for the candle to be completely burned down from first lighting was observed.

The three tests were conducted simultaneously.

Variables
Candle type: paraffin wax, soy wax, beeswax

Wick type: paper, cotton, wood

Observations

- The paraffin candle was the second to burn down completely

- The candle with the cotton wick burned for 80% of the time taken to burn the wood-wick candle

- The soy candle took the longest time to burn

- The wood-wick candle was not made of soy wax

Results

Candle type	Wick type	Burn time (1st = fastest)

NOT A TRICK
QUESTION

During a brief visit to a college cafeteria, Einstein happened to observe a mathematics professor who was discussing a student's end-of-year grade.

She had given the student a mark from 1 to 100, and had invited him to meet with her to discuss the grade in person. Instead of simply telling the student his grade directly, however, she set him a challenge.

She invited him to guess the grade she had given him. She would either say that the guess was correct, too high, or too low. If it was not correct, the student could continue to guess in the same way.

In the worst case, what is the minimum number of attempts needed for the student to able to guarantee that he can state the correct grade?

AS OLD AS TIME

Two physicists, a mother and daughter, had been working on a general relativity paper for several years, inspired by Einstein's own work.

At the beginning of the project, the daughter's age was four-ninths of that of her mother's.

When the project was finally complete—exactly eight years after they commenced work—the mother was now twice her daughter's age, plus one additional year.

As of the end of the project, what is the age difference between the two physicists?

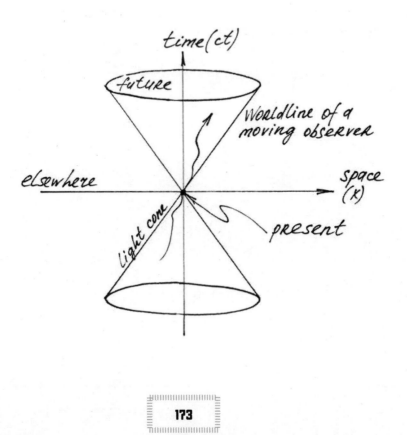

COAT TALES

A research facility had just received a bag full of clean lab coats, which had been sent away for laundering and then sterilizing.

Inside the bag were twelve coats, with each being one of three different sizes: small, medium, or large. There were an equal number of each size of lab coat.

A research team setting up for the day opened the bag to see that the sizes were randomly arranged and had no labels—in fact they were visually indistinct from one another when in the bag, due to the way they had all been folded.

The team of four needed two small lab coats, and two large ones. What is the minimum number of coats they would need to pull from the bag to be sure to have drawn out two of each?

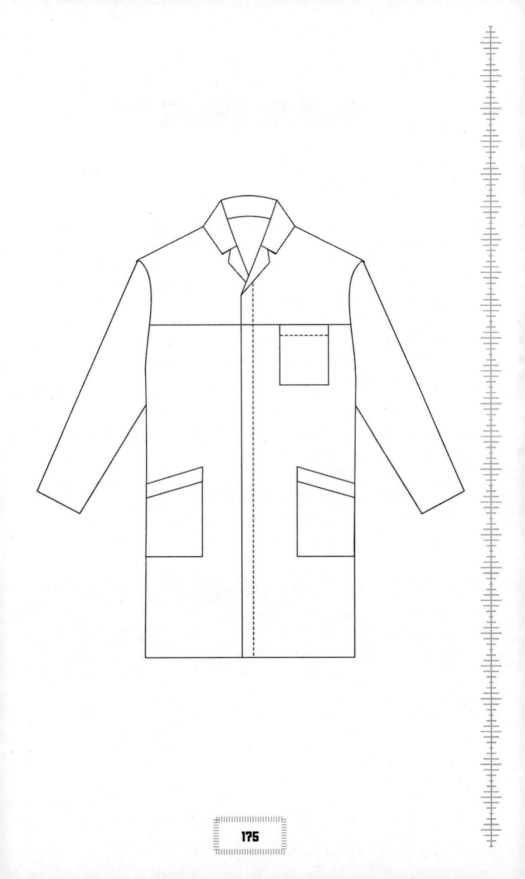

CHAIRING DECISION

A technician at Einstein's research institute was asked to arrange some chairs in a meeting room so that they would be suitably positioned for an upcoming presentation.

There were to be a total of five chairs in the room, and he was asked to arrange them so that all of the chairs were placed against a wall.

Also, he was asked to make sure that each wall had the same number of chairs against it as the wall opposite, so that the room did not feel unbalanced. The room was a usual rectangular shape.

Can it be done?

HOT OR COLD ICE

A physicist set the following question for his students to discuss:

If you were to go skating on a frozen lake surface, which of the following surfaces would be easier to skate on:

- One where the average temperature of the ice is -2°C

- One where the average temperature of the ice is -20°C

Which do you think it would be?

THE MAGIC EGG

Three of Einstein's more junior students were standing around in the university cafeteria, considering a question that was part physics and part culinary science.

They were discussing whether eggs float or sink when placed into water.

One of them said that a fresh, raw egg in its shell will normally sink when placed into a cup of water.

The other agreed that this was true, but said that it was possible to make it float.

A third then raised the stakes by saying that he also knew a way to make the egg float halfway between the bottom of a cup and the surface of the water.

How could the second and third students make an egg behave in this way?

SIMPLE SAILING

A student of physics was taking a short break from a particularly tricky problem, when he happened to sit and watch some model boats floating on a local lake.

This reminded him of a problem he had once been set back in his schooldays, as follows:

> If you have a model boat that is moved only by wind in its sails, but there is no wind, then would attaching a small battery-powered fan to the back of the boat—directed so that it blows wind into the sails—propel the boat forward?

BYE BYE, BIRDY

A series of experiments were being planned by a group of scientists in preparation for an upcoming space flight.

One of the group had suggested taking up small animals to see how they behaved in zero-gravity conditions.

To this end, another of the group suggested taking up a bird.

But then a third member said that even if you were to supply a bird with adequate water for the journey, it would soon die of dehydration in any case.

Why is this?

GETTING COLD FEET

The day before defending his dissertation, one of Einstein's PhD students expressed to his professor just how nervous he was about the big day, and that he was getting cold feet.

Einstein tried to diffuse his nerves by setting him the following physics poser:

> The central heating in your house is designed to make sure that it is the same temperature in every room, give or take a small amount due to varying convection currents and so forth.
>
> However, whenever you use the bathroom at night, you notice that the tiled floor of the bathroom is much colder on your bare feet than the carpeted floor of your bedroom and hallway.
>
> Why is this so?

Why indeed?

UPLIFTING RESULT

Discussing a recent near disaster, a group of physics students were pondering the series of events that had led to the avoidance of what would have been a particularly serious plane crash near the university campus.

As best they could gather from the local newspaper, the plane had stalled and then begun to plummet into a nosedive. The pilot had tried to pull out of the dive immediately, but was unsuccessful. After the plane had been nosediving for some time, however, the pilot tried again and this time he was able to pull out of the dive.

Why was it easier for him to pull out of a nosedive after the plane had been diving for some time?

TWO IN, ONE OUT

A particularly loud-mouthed member of the biology department was regaling the university cafeteria with a long-winded and particularly egocentric story about his recent adventures.

One of those present in the room remarked rather archly to the scientist next to him that it is sometimes said that you have two eyes and two ears but only one mouth—because you ought to look and listen more than you speak.

Putting aside the annoying loudmouth, what is the biological explanation for this phenomenon of two eyes, two ears but only one mouth?

THE COMPASS SHIFT EXPERIMENT

The following report on an experiment involving magnetic compasses is missing four entries from its results section. Can you fill them in correctly?

Abstract

A magnetic compass was tested in three distinct geographic locations to assess its accuracy.

Method

The same magnetic compass was tested in three different states across the United States to monitor accuracy and magnetic declination. The compass measurement was compared against existing isogonic charts, and against the celestial poles.

Each measurement was taken at the same height above sea level, in an outdoors location without any nearby large buildings or hills, and placed on the same horizontal mounting surface at each location.

Variables

States: Washington, Wisconsin, Maine

Towns: Arlington, Clinton, Franklin

Observations

The following compass readings were recorded at all three locations:

- The measurement taken in Franklin was inaccurate by 12°

- The measurement taken in Maine was four times as inaccurate as the one taken in Washington

- The most accurate reading was taken in Arlington, at 5° variation

- None of the readings was inaccurate by more than 30°

Results

1. The least accurate reading, of _____°, was taken in the town of _____ in the state of _____

2. The result showing 12° of inaccuracy was observed in the town of Franklin in the state of _____

H₂ OH NO

One of Einstein's assistants was enjoying a rare holiday and taking part in a scuba diving expedition.

She had swum a good way down to the bottom of the ocean and was examining some coral, when to her horror she realized that her oxygen tank had stopped working. In order to make it back to the surface, she had to swim upward rapidly, hoping that the air in her lungs was enough to get her all the way there.

Luckily she made it to the surface without suffering any harm, but as general advice should she have held her breath as she swam upward, or should she have gradually let the air escape from her mouth? She was not so deep that decompression sickness would affect her.

FLAT SPELUNKING

A group of hardy scientists were in the process of exploring a particularly deep cave system.

After several days of long and arduous travel, they succeeded in reaching the lowest point that anyone had ever reached.

To celebrate this momentous occasion, one of them had brought a small bottle of fizzy champagne to open. However, when they attempted to pop open the bottle, the cork remained resolutely in place. Even after they had opened it using some of the tools they had at their disposal, they were all still disappointed that the drink was completely flat.

Assuming that the champagne was not at fault, why did the drink not bubble as normal?

TEMPERATURE EXPERIMENT 3

A further set of thermometers has been carefully arranged to fill a square tray, as shown opposite. Each was set to measure the temperature of a particular substance, and the results were collated by writing various numbers outside the tray. The mercury was then drained out of each thermometer.

Can you shade in some or all of each thermometer to show the level the mercury reached in each thermometer during the experiment? Each number outside the tray shows the total number of grid squares in that row or column which should contain mercury. Each grid square is either entirely filled with mercury or entirely empty, and each thermometer must be filled from the bulb outward.

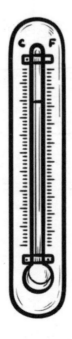

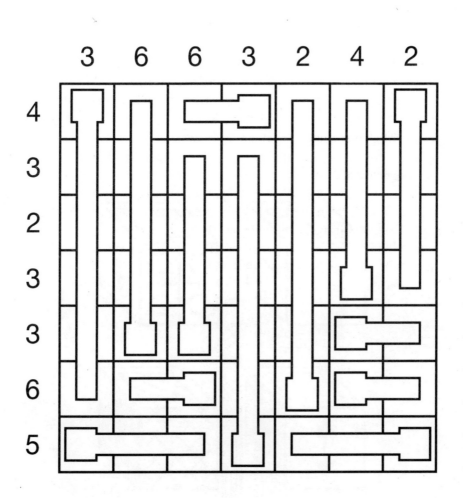

THE UNKNOWABLE CUBE 3

Two mathematicians were challenging one another to identify the properties of various solid cubes as quickly as possible, and were keeping track of who won the most races.

One of the challenges they set themselves was to work out which of the faces, "a" to "e" opposite, should replace the blank white face on the complete cube below?

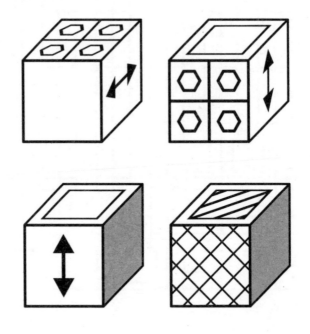

a.   b.   c.

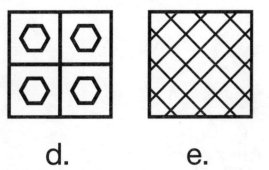

d.   e.

WINE WHINE

Einstein was attending a cocktail party to celebrate the launch of a book he had been heavily involved with.

While there, the chat inevitably turned to physics, with one attendee asking another the following question:

> "If I wet my finger and slide it round the rim of this wine glass at just the right speed, why does it start to make a singing noise?"

Why indeed does this happen? And why does your finger usually need to be wet for it to work?

WINTER WONDERING

Walking home from the lab one evening, after a particularly invigorating discussion with Einstein earlier in the day, one of his protégées felt herself wondering why it seemed so quiet.

All around the ground lay covered with recently fallen snow, and she wondered whether it was simply the association of snow with the festive season that made her feel that it was unusually peaceful.

There was, however, a more physics-based explanation as to why the snow made it seem quieter. What was it?

RADIO RESERVATION

After a recent radio interview, Einstein was complaining to some of his colleagues that he disliked the sound of his voice when he heard it played back via recordings. He noted that when he heard himself speak normally, when speaking directly, that he had no such concerns.

One of the colleagues wondered why this be, but of course quick as a flash the great man came back with an explanation of the likely physics behind the phenomenon.

What do you think Einstein said?

CRACKING CUBES

The chemists at Einstein's university were a convivial group, and were holding a social mixer to welcome the newest member of the team to the department.

The drinks that were being served were all at room temperature, however, so one of the team had made a quick detour to their lab to collect a bag of ice cubes.

When the ice cubes were added to the drinks, however, they made a loud cracking sound as they hit the liquid—as indeed ice cubes often do.

Can you explain why these loud cracks were heard?

THE BROWNIAN MOVEMENT EXPERIMENT

The following report on an experiment involving Brownian movement has just been submitted as part of an assignment. Three of the key words have been left blank, however. Can you fill them in correctly?

Abstract

Three liquids infused with foreign particles were examined under a microscope to measure the speed at which the particles moved through the liquid.

Method

5ml was extracted of each of three liquids and placed onto three observation slides, and left to rest for ten minutes. Then a fixed amount of foreign particles were introduced to each liquid and the resulting mixture observed under a microscope.

In order to ensure the experimenter was not influenced by pre-existing expectations, each liquid was assigned a code name by a third party and identified only by that name during the experiment.

Variables

Liquids: Clear oil; distilled water; ethanol

Code names: Phi; Rho; Nu

Observations

- The liquid code-named Phi had the fastest-moving particles

- The distilled water had the code name Nu

- The oil was observed to contain neither the fastest- nor the slowest-moving particles

Results

1. The _____ liquid had the fastest-moving foreign particles

2. The oil droplet was code-named _____

3. The droplet code-named _____ had the slowest-moving foreign particles

SOLUTIONS

PLAYING BALL **p.9**
The friend should spin the ball as fast as possible backward as they drop it. The contrasting airflow at the nearside of the ball, compared to the complementary airflow at the far side, would help drive the ball away from the building—and therefore hopefully avoid the stream. Alternatively, they could try to give the ball a slight inward motion in the hope that it would bounce off the building and travel away from the wall.

HOT AND COLD **p.10**
650g. The ice would weigh the same as the liquid water, despite now taking up more of the space in the container.

COMPARE AND CONTRAST **p.11**
Ingot A, which weighs 490g, as compared to ingot B, which weighs 480g.

BOOKMARKED FOR LATER **p.12**
The student could partially fold the bookmark and then drop it edge-side down. For example, if folded three times to form a square shape, it would have a good chance of landing with the square shape facing up.

THE RESEARCH FACILITY **p.14**
The South Pole. For six months of the year the sun does not rise at all.

HIDDEN SYMBOLS **p.15**
The word is "CAUTION," which can be found by replacing each word with its corresponding chemical symbol: C, Au, Ti, O, and N.

NOT AS EXTREME **p.17**
100 miles from the North Pole. For a circumference of 314 miles, the radius of the circle it flew around the North Pole must have been 50 miles, which is added to the initial 50 miles to give a total distance from the North Pole of 100 miles.

TIME TRAVELS **p.18**
The astronomer in question had made their first chart in 1478 BCE, and made more accurate ones 36 years later, in 1442 BCE.

SOLUTIONS

DISPERSION DIVERSION **p.21**

The second student. If the liquid levels in the flasks are the same as they were at the beginning of the experiment, then the amount of pink liquid displaced by the clear liquid in one flask must be exactly matched by the amount of pink liquid in the other flask.

THE GUEST LIST 1 . . . . **p.22**

Phoebe Ingles—there is no element with chemical symbol "Pi."

TEST CUBES **p.23**

Cube B—which weighs twice as much as cube A.
If each dimension of cube A is a in length, then its volume will be $a \times a \times a = a^3$. The volume of cube B will therefore be $2a \times 2a \times 2a = 8a^3$. Therefore, despite the fact that cube A is 4 times heavier for a piece of the same volume, cube B will be 8/4 = 2 times the weight of cube A.

THE DARK SIDE. **p.24**

It takes the moon the same time to spin once on its axis as it does to complete a single rotation around the earth, and both spin in the same direction. This means that only one side of the moon is ever visible from earth.

THE OBSERVERS OBSERVE. **p.25**

Yes, though it would not be possible for them to say *which* person it would be, nor that it would consistently be the same person.
It seems counterintuitive, but the person in question can simply be always referring to someone who is awake if not everyone is simultaneously asleep; or if everyone is asleep, it can be anyone who is asleep. So the statement is always true, if not very revelatory.

STUDENT AND SUPERVISOR **p.26**

84 minutes.
The student gains them 7 minutes, so in the 21 minutes elapsed he has washed as many beakers as the supervisor would have washed in 7 minutes. This means he is three times slower than the supervisor. Therefore if the supervisor would take 28 minutes to wash the beakers, and the student is three times as slow, it would take him $3 \times 28 = 84$ minutes.

SOLUTIONS

TWO ROVERS. **p.27**
One of the rovers should remain by the shore of the lake, and the other drive around the lake's perimeter. Once the second rover has completed a circle of the lake, the cord will be wrapped around the lost probe's mast, and the two rovers can then drive away from the lake to bring it back toward the shore.

THE DRAG RACE. **p.28**
The car would never complete the course. Although it would come very close, the halving of the distance completed at each interval means that it would never quite reach the finish line.

FRENCH CORRECTION. **p.29**
The Eiffel Tower is made of metal, which expands in the heat and so it "grows" around 15cm (6 inches) taller in summer.

SET THEORY 1. . . . . **p.30**
Set A—compounds including hydrogen: methane = CH_4 and ammonia = NH_3.
Set B—compounds including oxygen: carbon dioxide CO_2 and quicklime = CaO.
Set A + B—compounds with both hydrogen and oxygen: water = H_2O and ethanol = C_2H_5OH.

MAJESTIC MECHANICS. **p.31**
A quarter of the way around, at which point the turning coin would be upside down:

FLUID DYNAMICS. **p.33**
They could:

- Ensure all the fluid is drained into the bottom of each clock.
- Then, turn clocks A and B over at the same time.

- Next, turn over clock A once all the fluid has passed through, so it starts to time again.
- Finally, once clock A has finished for the second time, a total of 8 minutes will have passed, so they now have a way to time the exactly one minute until clock B finishes.

DRIP FEEDING 1 . . . . p.34
15 drops.
This is because a total of 120 drops of water were administered over the two minutes: 1 + 2 + 3 + ... + 14 + 15 = 120 drops = 120 seconds = 2 minutes.

GROWING PAINS p.35
Four days.
At the end of day 1 it is 30cm tall; by the end of day 2 it is 90cm tall; by the end of day 3 it is 270cm tall; and by the end of day 4 it is 810cm tall.

SEEING CLEARLY p.36
56 goggles.
Say the original cabinet could fit a goggles, then the new cabinet can fit $a + 16$. We also know that $a + 16 = a \times 140\% = 1.4a$. So $a + 16 = 1.4a$. If we subtract a from both sides, we see that $16 = 0.4a$. So $a = 40$, and therefore the new cabinet can fit $40 + 16 = 56$ goggles.

A SOLUTION p.37
By almost half, to about 500g.
The salt would not evaporate with the water, so for the salt proportion to double the water content needs to halve. In this case, just under 1l of water would need to become just under 500ml. As water has a unit density of 1 kg/l, half of the original weight would be approximately 500g.

ARTIFICIAL INTELLIGENCE p.39
Although the tether had been attached to the robot, it had not, unfortunately been attached at its other end. So the robot was able to travel any distance around the room, including over to the control computer.

NATURAL RESISTANCE p.40
The first pair of flights took longer. Although the headwind and tailwind may appear to cancel one another out, the headwind is acting on the plane for longer (since it is slowing the plane down) and the tailwind for less time, and therefore this makes the total journey time longer than if there had been no wind at all.

THE ATOMIC CLOCKS p.42

The correct sentences are as follows:

1. The clock using **mercury** as an element, code name **Xi**, was the most precise.

2. The clock using caesium as an element, code name **Mu**, was the least precise.

ATOMIC STRUCTURE p.44

There are 49 atoms in the arrangement: 4 at the very top, 13 on the layer below, and then 16 on each of the bottom two layers.

FAIR AND SQUARE p.46

The missing number is 9, since it is the only number in the range 1 to 15 not present, and it should be placed at the very beginning of the sequence shown. The mathematical logic is that all consecutive pairs of numbers add up to a square number. The only place that 9 could satisfy this condition is at the beginning of the sequence, since 9 + 7 = 16, a square number.

PRECISELY THE POINT p.48

She asked, "What time is it?"—or some similar question that involved measuring the current time.

IN ALL PROBABILITY p.49

1 in 5—there are initially 6 possible options, but one is removed once you know lithium has been picked. Using S for sodium, P for potassium, L1 for the first lithium container, and L2 for the second lithium container, they are L1+L2; L1+S; L1+P; L2+S; L2+P and S+P. After picking a lithium, S+P is removed as an option, so there is a 1 in 5 chance from the remaining options that he took both L1 and L2.

THE RUNNING TOTAL. p.50

None. They have perhaps only a few hours, since for this to be true they must have their realization on the day of the conference. If it's taken twice as long to work through only half of the fossils, then it must be the day of the conference already—in this case, ten days later.

SETTING UP CAMP p.53

6 astronomers (with 6 chairs), and 10 telescopes.

THE GUEST LIST 2 . . . . p.54

Jack and Quentin—the letters J and Q are not found in any chemical element symbol.

THE LOWEST OF THE LOW p.55
Mercury freezes at around -38°C, so a mercury thermometer would not function at -40°C.

DRIP FEEDING 2 .... p.56
The 10th flask.
The running totals are: 1 flask = 1 drop; 2 flasks = 3 drops; 3 flasks = 6 drops; 4 flasks = 10 drops; 5 flasks = 15 drops; 6 flasks = 21 drops; 7 flasks = 28 drops; 8 flasks = 36 drops; 9 flasks = 45 drops; 10 drops = 55 drops. So the 50th drop would go into the 10th flask.

CUBISM p.58
a. 6 cuts: The geologist should make 2 cuts equally spaced on one side; then rotate the cube 90 degrees in one dimension and make another 2 cuts; then rotate it 90 degrees in a different dimension and make a further 2 cuts.

b. No: Because cubes are required, it is not possible to reduce the number of cuts.

c. Yes: If any shape was acceptable then, with rearrangement between cuts, the number of pieces could be doubled at each cut and in which case there could be as many as 32 pieces after 5 cuts.

DRONING ON p.59
The student, who will fly the drone for 400m farther than their supervisor
The distance the drone flies out is $x + 500m$. On the way back, the distance flown is $x + 200m + 300m$. The supervisor flies $x + 300m$, while the student flies $x + 500m + 200m = x + 700m$. So the student flies it 400m farther.

THE CAKE IS A LIE p.60
Two of the group were both a student *and* a supervisor.
For example, there may be a PhD supervisor; their PhD student, who is also supervising a masters student; their masters student, who is also supervising an undergraduate; the undergraduate.

ROCK, PAPER, MINERAL p.61
From most to least prevalent: calcite, dolomite, serpentine, silica, alumina.

A ROCK AND A HARD PLACE................................. p.62
He should take all but one of the diamonds from the diamond bag and add them to the bag of fake gems. Now if he chooses the diamond bag when blindfolded (a 50%

chance), he has a 100% chance of retrieving a diamond. If he picks the other bag, he has a 9/19 chance of picking out a diamond, or roughly 47.4%. The overall odds of picking a diamond therefore become approximately 73.7%. This is much better than the default 50:50 odds he would have had.

UPSIDE DOWN. p.64
The postcard. Both the Norwegian flag and the eight of diamonds are likely to look identical when inverted upside-down, but the Eiffel tower would not.

DOING IT BY HALVES p.65
Victor's.

CONSTELLATION CONUNDRUM p.66
Appropriately, the ten stars could be arranged in the formation of a five-pointed star, with a star at each point and each intersection of imaginary connecting lines as shown:

CAN YOU DIG IT. p.69
He could dig earth from inside the trench to create a slope that he could use to climb out.

TWO BY TWO p.70
Two dollars.
On boarding each ferry the passenger would hand over one of the dollars, and then get the same dollar back when leaving. So they would both start and end with two dollars, and therefore spend nothing for all six ferries.

SMASHING STUFF p.72
30 test tubes.
For the second technician's statement to be true, it must be that between them a full box worth of test tubes is smashed.

POUR PERFORMANCE p.73
The technician can fill up the 300ml flask and pour it into the 700ml flask, then do this a second time so there is now 600ml in the 700ml flask. Next they should fill the 300ml flask a third time and use it to fill the remaining 100ml of space in the 700ml flask, leaving 200ml in the 300ml beaker. They can then completely empty

SOLUTIONS

the 700ml beaker and pour in the 200ml. Now if they fill the 300ml beaker again, they can also pour this into the 700ml beaker to give a resulting total of 500ml.

TIME TO REFLECT 1 . . . . p.74
Image "b"

CHEMISTRY COMPARISON p.76
21: 7 gases, 2 liquids and 12 solids.
The 12 solids and 2 liquids described make 14. We also know that a third of the containers hold gases so 14 must be two-thirds of the total. $14 \times 3 \div 2 = 21$.

TEAM TALK p.77
Yes—and there would be five extra people.
If the first researcher was male and the second was female, and the group of people working with them consisted of an additional two males and three females, this would be true.

SHARE IT OUT p.78
One of the scientists had been given the briefcase with the final rock sample still inside it.

CIRCULAR DEFINITION p.79
48.
This is easiest to see if we subtract 8 from both numbers, which we can do since the dishes are evenly spaced, referring to them instead as the 0th and 24th petri dish. The 24th dish is opposite the 0th, so it must be halfway round, meaning there are 48 dishes in total.

SHINE BRIGHT p.80
Alpha produced 530 lumens, and Beta 470.

STATISTICALLY SPEAKING p.81
Yes.
Say for example that 24 students in a class of 32 each answered 10 questions, and the remaining 8 each answered 2 questions, then the average number of questions answered would be $(24 \times 10 + 8 \times 2) \div 32 = 8$. Any students answering 9 or more questions would therefore have answered an above-average number, and 24 out of 32 is indeed 75% of the students.

SOLUTIONS

HEADS UP **p.82**

Whoever would normally choose "heads" or "tails" should instead call "heads then tails" or "tails then heads". They should keep tossing the coin in discrete pairs of flips, until a pair of flips contains two different results and then act accordingly.

Whatever the weighting of the coin, the chances of getting heads and then tails is the same as getting tails and then heads, when given a pair of flips. Of course, the chance of getting two results the same on the biased side is much higher, and the chance of getting two results the same on the unbiased side is much lower, but these results are ignored.

THE VETERAN **p.83**

Sample A had been gathered 36 years ago, and sample B had been gathered 18 years ago.

ADD AND MULTIPLY **p.84**

3 in the 1st year, 2 in the 2nd year and 1 in the 3rd year.

The agency must have sent 1 astronaut one year, 2 in another year and 3 in another: $1 + 2 + 3 = 1 \times 2 \times 3 = 6$. Given the ordering in the question, this must be 3, 2 and 1 astronauts respectively.

THE MIX-UP **p.86**

Test a vial from the shelf marked "ACID OR ALKALI." We know this isn't the mixed shelf, since all the labels are wrong, so if it's acidic then the shelf labelled "ACID" (which is wrong too) must have alkali vials, and the "ALKALI" shelf must have the mix of vials. Or if it's alkaline, then the opposite must be true: the "ALKALI" shelf must have only acid vials.

THE LOSING LECTURER **p.87**

No.

For Einstein to have played only five games out of eleven, given the rules as stated, he must have started playing in the second game and lost every game he played—since he could not have "stayed on" to play a consecutive game.

THE UNKNOWABLE CUBE 1 . . . . **p.88**

Face "d"

ELEMENTAL DIGITS **p.90**

A mirror.

If held horizontally across the middle of the numbers, a mirror would produce a

SOLUTIONS

reflection that appeared to show the letters O, B, H, and I, which are the chemical symbols for each of the listed elements: O=oxygen, B=boron, H=hydrogen, I=iodine.

INSTITUTIONAL INDICATOR p.91
11 years.

The first square number where the first and third digits are equal is 121, so the combined age is 121 years. If one is 10 × older than the other, then its age is 10/11ths of 121. Since 10 ÷ 11 × 121 = 110, it must be 110 years old, meaning the other must be 11 years old.

THE LOST BRIEFCASES p.92

- The biochemist left their briefcase, which contained a test tube, in the cafeteria.

- The analytical chemist left their briefcase, which contained a microscope, in the library.

- The inorganic chemist left their briefcase, which contained a conical flask, in the modern languages department.

THE DOCTORAL PAPERS p.94

1. The quantum mechanics thesis, dedicated to Bohr.

2. Planck.

WEIGHING IT UP p.95
20g.

If the weight of a test tube is t, then $6t = t + 100$, so $5t = 100$ and therefore $t = 20$.

TEMPERATURE EXPERIMENT 1 .... p.96

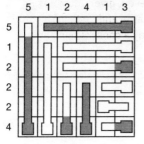

SOLUTIONS

IT TAKES TWO TO MANGO p.98
Count the number of mango stones which had been cut out, as they wouldn't have been added to the container for pulping and would be very unlikely to have been cut into multiple pieces.

REACTION TIME p.99
They could tip the beaker at an angle, stopping just at the moment that any liquid would pour out if they were to tip it further. If any of the flat bottom of the beaker was visible at that point, then it would be less than half full. This is true because it was a perfect cylinder.

COMPOSITE IMAGE 1 . . . . p.100
6.
The six-pointed stars are indicated with shading here:

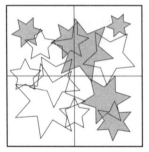

ASTRONOMICAL ODDS. p.103
36.
The first scientist named 19 stars, the second named 7, and the third and fourth named 5 each. To deduce this, start by working out that the fourth person named 5 stars, then work backward person by person from there.

THE DOCTORAL DUO p.104
Ava was 54 and Ben was 27.
If a and b are their current ages, then $a = 2b$. We also know that $b - 6 = 3/7 (a - 5)$. Substituting $2b$ for a in the second equation gives $b - 6 = 3/7 (2b - 5)$. Expanding the bracket, this rearranges to $b = 6/7b - 15/7 + 6$. If we multiply both sides by 7, we have $7b = 6b - 15 + 42$. Subtracting $6b$ from both sides gives $b = 27$. So $a = 54$.

SOLUTIONS

STAR SLIDES 1 . . . . p.105
d. LSA.
The code is as follows, for each letter in the code in turn:

1. For the five-pointed star: L = points up; M = points down

2. For the four-pointed star: S = shaded; T = white

3. For the five-pointed star: A = shaded; B = white

OFFICIAL SECRETS 1 . . . . p.106
Nation A should place the document in the case and then send it, with their
padlock attached, to nation B. Upon receipt, nation B should also attach their
own padlock and send it back to nation A, who should remove their own padlock.
Nation A can then send it back to nation B with B's padlock attached—which nation
B can then unlock safely.

THE LONG AND SHORT OF IT p.109
Due to a lack of gravitational pull on the astronaut's spine, he had become about
3% taller than on earth as the soft tissue between their bones expanded. Similarly,
on earth humans may be 1cm or so shorter at the end of each day compared to at
the beginning of the day, after sleeping horizontally.

CONFOUNDING COMPOUNDS 1 . . . . p.110

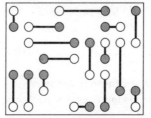

RELATIVE BRILLIANCE p.111

SOLUTIONS

THE ACADEMIC LUNCH **p.112**

1. The quantum theorist was drinking orange cordial
2. The tea-drinker was from the University of Tokyo
3. The professor from Princeton was a molecular biologist

A SIGN OF WIND **p.115**
He could stand it back up and point the arm for the station in the correct direction, which he would know since he had entered the site here from the station. At this point the remaining arm should point him where he wished to go.

SET THEORY 2 . . . . **p.116**
Set A: elements with atomic numbers which are square numbers.
Set B: elements with atomic numbers which are cube numbers.
Set A + B: elements with atomic numbers which are both square numbers and cube numbers.

TAKE YOUR SEATS **p.117**
50:50.
This is true no matter how many people are in line to take their seats.

DOUBLE DISCOVERY **p.118**
The discoveries were made at 23:30 on 28th February, and 00:30 on 1st March. The decade celebration was held during a leap year, where the two would be separated by an intervening 24 hours on 29th February.

ROBOT RACE **p.121**
Yes, by just over one second.
The slower robot took $54/90 \times 100 = 60$ seconds to finish the course. This means that the slower robot travels at $50m \div 60s = 0.83$ m/s. Over a distance of $50m - 4m = 46m$ it will therefore take $46 \div 0.83 = 55.2$ s. So it would take 1.2 seconds longer to reach the finish line.

SOLUTIONS

CONFOUNDING COMPOUNDS 2 . . . . p.122

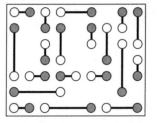

RULE WITH A ROD OF IRON p.123
He could pick up one of the rods and touch its end to the middle of the other bar. If the magnetized bar is the one which has been picked up, it will attract the other bar. If the two are not attracted, then it is the non-magnetized bar which has been picked up, since magnetic rods have two poles so are magnetic at either end—but not in the middle.

PEAK BEAKER p.124
There would be ten beakers the right way up.
Reading along the row, beakers 1, 4, 9, 16, 25, 36, 49, 64, 81, and 100 would be the right way up. This is because these are square numbers, meaning they have an odd number of factors—therefore they would be turned over an odd number of times. All the other numbers have an even number of factors, so would be turned over an even number of times and therefore end up back as they started: upside down.

TIME TO REFLECT 2 . . . . p.125
Image "d".

THE UNFORTUNATE PARTY p.127
If whatever was causing the illness was trapped in the ice, then early on in the party there might have been very little of the virus in the water, but it may then have been progressively released into the container as the ice melted. Anyone who only drank early on might then have avoided exposure.

THE COMPOUND EXPERIMENT p.128

Liquid code name	Identified liquid	Identified formula
Zeta	Ethanol	C_2H_6O
Iota	Sulfuric acid	H_2SO_4
Psi	Acetic acid	$C_2H_4O_2$

SOLUTIONS

OVER THE MOONS **p.131**
36.
The number of moons in A + C = 45, and we know that A = 1/4 C. So 1/4C + C = 45,
meaning C = 36. Therefore photo A showed 9 moons, B showed 22 moons, and C
showed 36, which is the greatest number that could be confirmed if the moons in
A and B were each subsets of those in photo C.

MANY MOONS **p.132**

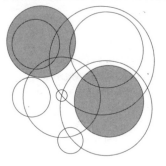

TAKING SIDES **p.133**
If you were to sit inside the corner of a large opaque cube, you could move your
eyes to see parts of all six interior faces without having to move either the cube or
your body.

THE UNKNOWABLE CUBE 2 . . . . **p.134**
Face "a".

KEEP IT ON FILE **p.136**
He could use a magnet. The iron filings will be attracted to the magnet, but the
titanium filings would not.

ON YOUR MARKS **p.137**
360 papers.
6 papers per day for 6 people for 10 days = 10 × 6 × 6 = 360 papers

SOLUTIONS

TEMPERATURE EXPERIMENT 2 . . . . **p.138**

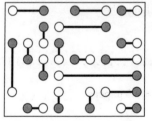

THE SHUTTLE SHUFFLE **p.141**

If each physicist lives one stop from the end of the line, the shuttle will spend a relatively small amount of time in the area between the stop and the end of the route, compared to the time it spends on the remainder of the route. Therefore if the physicist arrives randomly at the bus stop, it is far more likely the bus will be on the side away from the end of the route—and therefore first seen heading in the wrong direction.

STAR SLIDES 2 . . . . **p.142**

e. QDX.

The code is as follows, for each letter from left to right:

1. F = shaded star; Q = white star

2. R = planet in front of star; D = planet behind star

3. W = planet at top right; X = planet at bottom left

CONFOUNDING COMPOUNDS 3 . . . . **p.143**

SOLUTIONS

THE BOILING POINTS EXPERIMENT p.144

1. X's boiling point: 95°C
2. Y's boiling point: 36°C
3. Z's boiling point: 72°C

UPS AND DOWNS p.147

The first professor should take thirteen papers from his pile, create a second pile with these thirteen papers, and then flip the entire pile upside down.

The new pile and the old pile will now have the same number of face-up essays, no matter how many were taken from the original pile. This is because if there are 13 face up in the original single pile, there will now be 13 - n in that pile after removing some, where n is the number of face-up papers removed for the new pile. But with 13 papers in the new pile, if this is now flipped then it will change from having n face-up papers to *also* contain 13 - n face-up papers. So both piles now have 13 - n face-up papers.

TIME FOR CHANGE p.148

Three quarters (25¢), one dime (10¢), two nickels (5¢), and five cents.

SET THEORY 3 .... p.150

Set A: units of measurement named after people.
Set B: Nobel Prize winners.
Set A + B: units of measurement named after Nobel Prize winners.

CUMULATIVE CHEMISTRY p.151

Day 10, where he would set up tanks 89 to 143.
The number of tanks added each day, with running totals, is as follows: 1, + 1 = 2, + 2 = 4, + 3 = 7, + 5 = 12, + 8 = 20, + 3 = 33, + 21 = 54, + 34 = 88, + 55 = 143

BY THE BOOK p.152

The meteorology book—for which they now owed $12.80, as opposed to $9 for the astrophysics book.
The amounts owed after each day are as follows: $1/$0.05; $2/$0.10; $3/$0.20; $4/$0.40; $5/$0.80; $6/$1.60; $7/$3.20; $8/$6.40; $9/$12.80.

SOLUTIONS

SUMS OF STEEL **p.153**

75cm.

Any cut to the 1m-long rod can be considered to always be at a point between 50cm and 100cm of its original span. If not, the rod could be flipped over before cutting so this was so. Given that mathematically the average place for that cut—if made randomly—must be in the middle of this 50cm length, then this must be at the 75cm mark. The longer piece will therefore average 75cm in length.

THE SOLAR ECLIPSE EXPERIMENT **p.154**

1. The Delta team were positioned in Italy.

2. The Gamma team were positioned in Brazil.

3. Intermittent cloud was observed by the Alpha team.

TIME TO REFLECT 3 . . . . **p.156**

"d".

HIDDEN STAR **p.157**

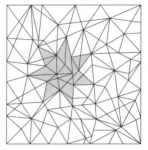

COMPOSITE IMAGE 2 . . . . **p.158**

11

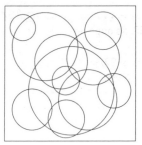

SOLUTIONS

STEP BY STEP **p.160**

70. The number of possible routes to any grid square is the sum of the number of possible routes to the grid squares to its left and below it:

1	5	15	35	70
1	4	10	20	35
1	3	6	10	15
1	2	3	4	5
⬡	1	1	1	1

IT'S A REAL KNOCKOUT **p.163**

64 players, with four rounds played.

In round one there are 32 matches between 64 players; in round two there are 16 matches; in round three there are 8 matches; then 4 matches; then 2 matches; then 1 final match. This gives the total of 32 + 16 + 8 + 4 + 2 + 1 = 63 matches.

IT'S A HYPOTHETICAL KNOCKOUT **p.164**

a. The first round, if they play player 1 in that round.

b. 8: player 1 could play player 9.

OFFICIAL SECRETS 2 . . . . **p.165**

8732.

MIRROR, MIRROR **p.166**

The mirrors were facing one another when installed.

A SHORT NOTE **p.168**

All of the "words" are in fact chemical element symbols. In order, they are: "Er" = erbium, "No" = nobelium; "As" = arsenic, "I" = iodine, "Am" = americium, "At" = astatine, "Be" = beryllium, "He" = helium, and "In" = indium.

STAR SLIDES 3 . . . . **p.169**

c. LDY.

The letters have the following meaning. All those that apply are listed in size order, from largest to smallest:

- J = star at the top right

- O = star at the bottom left

SOLUTIONS

- L = star at the bottom right
- N = star at the top left
- D = shaded object present
- E = black object present
- Y = white object present

THE CANDLE WICKING EXPERIMENT p.170

Candle type	Wick type	Burn time (1st = fastest)
Beeswax	Cotton	1st
Paraffin wax	Wood	2nd
Soy wax	Paper	3rd

NOT A TRICK QUESTION p.172

The minimum number of guesses required in the worst case is seven.
At each guess, the student should divide the grade space in half. Therefore they start by guessing 50 which, if not correct, will eliminate half of the possible grades. They should then continue suggesting the number halfway between the current closest guesses until they have the correct one—which will be in 7 guesses or fewer. In the worst case, the number of grades still available to guess after each attempt is as follows: 50; 25; 13; 7; 4; 2; 1. Of course, it might well be that their grade is only likely to be within a smaller range of values, so perhaps the strategy could be adapted in this particular situation.

AS OLD AS TIME p.173

45 years: when the project finished, they were 89 and 44.
If the daughter is now d years old, and the mother m years old, then now $m = 2d + 1$. We also know that $4/9(m - 8) = d - 8$, which can be rewritten as $4m/9 - 32/9 = d - 8$; and then as $4m - 32 = 9d - 72$; which means $4m = 9d - 40$, so $m = 9d/4 - 10$. Substituting into the first equation, $9d/4 - 10 = 2d + 1$, and therefore $9d - 40 = 8d + 4$, and so $d = 44$. This means that $m = 89$.

COAT TALES p.174

Ten.
There are four of each size, so in the worst case they draw all four medium lab coats, all four of one of the other sizes, and then finally two of the remaining size they need—for a total of ten.

SOLUTIONS

CHAIRING DECISION **p.176**

Yes. Place one of the five chairs in a corner, then two chairs on one of the walls opposite that corner and one chair on the other wall opposite the corner, and finally one chair on the wall between the corner and the wall with one chair. This can be seen here:

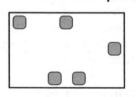

HOT OR COLD ICE **p.177**

It would be easier to skate on ice that is -2°C because at this temperature it would be possible for your skates to temporarily melt the ice as you skate over it, creating a lubricating layer of water. At -20°C it's too cold for this to happen, so there will be considerably more friction.

THE MAGIC EGG **p.178**

The second student knew that if they stirred salt into the water it would increase the density and the egg would then float near the top. The third student proposed to half fill the cup with salted water, float the egg on the top, and then slowly (to prevent them mixing) pour clean water on top—leaving the egg suspended in the middle.

SIMPLE SAILING **p.179**

No, probably not, since the fan would most likely propel the boat backward. This is partially because most of the wind created by the fan would most likely not be caught by the sails, thus outweighing the forward propulsion of the wind hitting the sails. In addition, the fan would also push itself in a backward direction too, which would also act upon the boat.

BYE BYE, BIRDY **p.180**

Birds have a gravity-based system for swallowing liquid. Luckily, human anatomy works differently in this respect! But without gravity, a bird would not be able to drink.

GETTING COLD FEET **p.181**

This apparent difference is explained by conduction. Carpet is a much worse conductor of heat than tiles, so when you step on the carpet it is slower to remove heat from your feet than tiles are, meaning it feels notably warmer.

SOLUTIONS

UPLIFTING RESULT p.182

In this case, as is common, the stalling was due to the plane moving too slowly, resulting in a lack of lift. The faster the plane dived, the more air flowed over the wings, until there was enough lift to enable the pilot to pull out of the dive.

TWO IN, ONE OUT p.183

Two eyes allow for depth perception and help you estimate distances, while two ears help you determine where a sound is coming from. Conversely, there is no such advantage to having two mouths.

THE COMPASS SHIFT EXPERIMENT p.184

1. The least accurate reading, of 20°, was taken in the town of Clinton in the state of Maine.

2. The result showing 12° of inaccuracy was observed in the town of Franklin in the state of Wisconsin.

H$_2$OH NO. p.186

Although you might think you should hold as much air in your lungs as possible to make you more buoyant, she should nonetheless have gradually let the air escape her mouth as she swam upward. This is because as she swam upward the pressure on her body would have decreased and the air in her lungs expanded. To avoid rupturing her lungs, it was best to gradually release that air. Of course, if you were only a very short distance beneath the surface, this would not be relevant.

FLAT SPELUNKING. p.189

The high air pressure far below the ground had kept the carbon dioxide in the champagne in solution, so it did not fizz.

TEMPERATURE EXPERIMENT 3 .... p.190

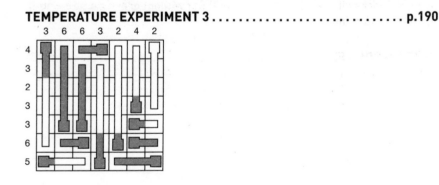

SOLUTIONS

THE UNKNOWABLE CUBE 3 . . . . p.192
Face "b".

WINE WHINE p.195
The wine glass will resonate at a particular frequency. Your finger causes the glass to vibrate until eventually the vibrations reach the natural frequency of the glass, which is when the glass makes the singing noise. Your finger usually needs to be wet to reduce friction sufficiently for it to be able to reach the glass's resonant frequency.

WINTER WONDERING p.196
Snow absorbs sound. Loosely packed snow in particular contains a large number of air gaps, causing it to act somewhat like the air gaps in double glazing that also absorb sound. It also makes it more difficult for sound to bounce off the snow than many other surfaces.

RADIO RESERVATION p.198
Einstein was used to hearing his voice inside his head, when it was audible through the vibrations of his skull. This gave it a lower sound than when he heard it through his ears, which was how other people were used to hearing it—or indeed as it would be heard when played back via an audio recording.

CRACKING CUBES p.199
The drinks were warmer than the ice that was added. When the ice cubes were dropped in, the outside of each cube warmed up rapidly and expanded, whereas the inside did not immediately do so. This tension causes the ice to crack, making the loud sounds heard.

THE BROWNIAN MOVEMENT EXPERIMENT p.200
1. The ethanol liquid had the fastest-moving foreign particles.
2. The oil droplet was code-named Rho.
3. The liquid code-named Nu had the slowest-moving foreign particles.